This insightful and engaging book t. journey of self-discovery, awareness, and transformation. Filled with supportive and useful exercises, *Beyond Divorce* will help ease the pain of the divorce experience by providing opportunities for growth, understanding, and transcendence.

—Christine A. Coates, J.D. co-author of *Learning from Divorce: How to Take Responsibility, Stop the Blame, Move On.*

Beyond Divorce provides concrete steps for getting onto a path of healing, understanding, and optimism in the wake of the personal storm that is a divorce. Jeannine Lee writes gently and kindly, encouraging our wounded selves to look inward—and within ourselves is the only place we can truly nurture change. Lee provides guidance with shifts in thinking, writing exercises, and alternate modes of behaving that can create new and more joyful ways of being in the world. This is a great book for all who are ready to embrace the full spectrum of being human.

—Tamara K. Vincelette, esq.

Jeannine offer lots—and I mean *lots*—of specific, concrete understanding of what makes divorce hurt and what we need to make things better sooner. Spend time with this book if you are devastated. Even if you aren't devastated, but something just doesn't feel right and you haven't been feeling like yourself, you will find significant value here.

—Michael K. Travers Jr., M.A., J.D., mediator and counselor at law

Jeannine Lee is a dedicated expert at helping people find peace after divorce. As a divorce attorney who has been divorced twice and been saved by divorce recovery classes, I recommend that everyone contemplating divorce, in the middle of divorce, or struggling to find happiness after divorce, read this book as it contains the secrets you desperately need. This book is amazing. You could not find a better resource for healing divorce trauma.

—Terri Harrington, esq. Denver Center for Mediation & Collaborative Law

Beyond Divorce offers those experiencing a breakup both a harbor in the storm and a light at the end of the tunnel. I recommend *Beyond Divorce* to my divorce clients as I believe all going through this painful time can benefit from Jeannine's well-informed and heartfelt approach. There is life "Beyond Divorce." It is critical that folks wading through the darkness learn how to build a new life for themselves.

—Sara L. Keane Ross, divorce attorney

Beyond Divorce provides an intuitive, compassionate, and practical approach to life after divorce. It encourages the reader to look deep within to find the courage and strength to manage the confusion and overwhelming emotions of divorce. Between these covers readers will find insight, wisdom, and tools to move out of pain and into a life of their choosing.

—Georgiana R. Scott, divorce attorney

Beyond Divorce is a must-read for anyone in the swirl of divorce. It provides a variety of tools to help calm the emotions and provide clarity, allowing the reader to make critical financial decisions from a place of reason rather than emotion.

—Tara Mohr, Certified Divorce Financial Analyst, CFP

The best description for this book is expansive. It covers the full scope of getting beyond divorce. Jeannine's compassion and non-judgment for your difficult feelings comes through. It's clear that she understands all sides of divorce whether you were the heartbroken or the heartbreaker, and whether your primary emotion is grief, anger, guilt, or some combination. The many exercises are profoundly effective in helping you cope, heal, and grow through and past, this difficult life change.

—Dane Schnal, class participant

My 15-year marriage ended painfully. I was deeply confused. After reading *Beyond Divorce*, and attending the companion 10-week program, I was able to move forward in my life, both in and out of relationships. I know that the best of my life is now ahead of me instead of behind.

—Christopher Young, class participant

Beyond Divorce™

STOP THE PAIN,
REKINDLE YOUR HAPPINESS,
AND PUT PURPOSE BACK
IN YOUR LIFE

Jeannine Lee

www.deliberatepress.com

Beyond Divorce: Stop the Pain, Rekindle Your Happiness,
and Put Purpose Back in Your Life

© 2014 by Jeannine Lee

Published by Deliberate Press, Ltd., Boulder, Colorado

Beyond Divorce™

ISBN-13: 978-0-9893541-0-3 (paperback)

ISBN-13: 978-0-9893541-1-0 (eBook: ePub)

ISBN-13: 978-0-9893541-2-7 (eBook: Kindle / mobi)

Printed in the United States

Cover art: © istockphoto.com/MandarineTree
Photo manipulation by RD Studio

Book design by DesignForBooks.com

To obtain other permissions,
contact info@DeliberatePress.com.

Contents

Part 3 Resolving the Emotions

Part 4 Managing Your Thoughts

Part 5 Learning from What Went Wrong

Part 6 Reclaiming Your Power

Part 7 Future Relating

Part 8 Looking Forward

Thank You

I wish to express gratitude to the many people who have encouraged me in the long and arduous journey of bringing this book to life. You told me just what I needed to hear when I was ready to give up, you provided feedback when I could no longer see clearly, you inspired me with your stories of the ways I've helped you heal your lives, and you have continued to support this transformational work.

I am grateful to my husband, Scott—who has spent many hours watching me write when he'd rather we be doing something else—for his unwavering confidence in my vision and for reminding me of it when I'd lost sight of it.

I'm grateful for the support of my children, who weren't sure just what Mom was up to but wanted to support it anyway, just because they're great kids.

Thanks to my parents and brothers who were always curious about my progress and cheerfully supported the project in their unique ways. Special thanks to my brother Scott for his encouragement and contributions on the creative end of the cover design.

Thank you to the many professionals who contributed their unique gifts: Jasmin Cori, Priscilla Stuckey, and Kathleen Erickson as editors, Michael Rohani for insight and guidance in the publishing process and patiently working with my inexperience as we developed the cover and interior design, and David Steele for helping me settle on a title and providing mentoring through the trademark process.

Thanks to other supporters: Dave Taylor for his insights with media marketing and development, Rob Gregg for all the fireside chats around the direction of this work, Dane Schnal for coming up with a great subtitle and very useful cover design input, Jaci Hull for her collegial encouragement, and Chris York for freely providing support and feedback on anything I've needed—on this project or any other. A special note of thanks to Todd Fisher who has been an enthusiastic supporter and champion of my work. Thank you to all the assistant helpers in our live classes who bring heart and compassion to every divorcing person. Your value is immeasurable.

I am indebted to each and every divorce recovery participant who has shared his or her life and story with me. Mark Twain once said: *"There was never yet an uninteresting life. Inside of the dullest exterior there is a drama, a comedy, and a tragedy."* Divorce is mostly a tragedy, loaded with drama, and it takes great humor to get through it. The lives of the divorcing reflect them all. I've seen people take the shambles of their lives and put them back together piece by piece into something better, stronger, and more vital than they ever imagined possible. I've seen people of all ages face their fears, develop necessary life skills, build new friendships, and create a new life for themselves. I am profoundly grateful to know every one of you. You inspire me each and every day.

Foreword

I am pleased to highly recommend *Beyond Divorce* by Jeannine Lee. I consider Jeannine the person most aptly suited as a successor to my father and his work on helping people recover after divorce.

My father, Bruce Fisher, was the man behind the book *Rebuilding When Your Relationship Ends*. From the early 1980s until his passing in 1998, he taught courses and seminars out of his home in Boulder, Colorado. I worked alongside him in several of those classes, coming to understand more deeply what he was trying to accomplish. It was clear to me that my father was motivated much more by his wish to help others than by any desire for monetary reward or interest in fame. He was instrumental in the transformation of people's lives and in helping them create new life from shattered dreams. More than one person has told me that he saved their lives.

After my father's death, many groups and individuals took up the mantle of teaching the Fisher courses. However, in the years since his death, much focus and direction in the work have been lost. Thus I am exceedingly motivated to support Jeannine, who imparts the heart and spirit of my father's work.

I became acquainted with Jeannine some years ago, first by phone and then in person. In speaking with her, I realized the calmness of her spirit and what I can only describe as the essence of an old soul. She is patient, compassionate, authentic, and very direct. Beneath her quiet confidence lies a steely determination, an "I am going to get this done" attitude that serves well the divorcing population she cares so much about.

Jeannine has a firm grasp on the importance of positive human interaction, complete communication, and mutual respect between people, which contributes to her effectiveness in helping people navigate their relationship endings. She has taken a parallel path to my father's work and has moved beyond it with her own style. She exemplifies the intent my father brought to his work better than anyone I know.

In looking through *Beyond Divorce*, I am impressed with the clarity, completeness, and compassion that she brings to the work. I highly recommend that people whose relationships are ending read this work and that they explore the teachings that Jeannine makes available on her website. She has been teaching in the Boulder area for some years now and has strong roots in the community.

Thank you for reading *Beyond Divorce*. I trust you will enjoy the teachings that Jeannine Lee has shared and that you will find hope and healing for your own journey.

Todd Fisher
West Richland, Washington
December 2012

Introduction

Ending a relationship is always painful, whether you were married for thirty years or experienced a captivating, intense, whirlwind of a relationship for a short time. Divorce is an experience of the heart. That holds true for both same-sex and opposite-sex couples. You may not be involved in a legal divorce if you weren't legally wed, but you will still experience the same emotional process, and that process is the focus of this book. Emotional pain is the same for everyone. It is the most unbearable of all pains. There is no morphine for emotional pain.

If you wanted the relationship to end, you can remember what wasn't working. Perhaps you carried the financial burden or the emotional load, or both, and you just can't do it anymore. Maybe you felt that continuing to stay in your relationship was a waste of time and life was passing you by. Perhaps you were forced to end the relationship because your partner just wasn't showing up, had an addiction, or was habitually unemployed. For whatever reason, you had to pull the plug.

If you were the one left behind, you are probably shocked, in disbelief, like a deer in the headlights. *"What happened? Sure, we had our problems, but I didn't think they were so bad we would divorce."*

However it ended, whether you wanted it or whether you didn't, it will take some effort to regroup and rebuild before you can re-envision your life.

Chances are that you did not get married anticipating that your love would one day evaporate and your marriage would end in divorce. (Although some people have a sneaking suspicion right from the start that the person they are marrying isn't the right one for them.) You got married for the long haul, for companionship, to have a partner in your old age. You got married for the happy-ever-after. And that is gone. You are alone again.

I know you are here for help to get through your divorce, and we will definitely provide that in some creative and powerful ways, but first I want you to see that there is a bigger picture. I don't want you to go through your divorce just to create what you had before. I want you to seize this opportunity—to heal, learn, grow, and garner the skills you need to create something greater. To leap out of the box you've lived in and create a life *beyond* current possibilities.

It is important to understand that losses are part of our movement through life. In the big picture, they alert us that another leg of our journey toward a more authentic version of self has begun. To use an agricultural analogy,

the old and the lifeless are being pruned away so you can bear more fruit.

What is left is strong and vital, the stuff from which your new life will be made. We experience many of these transitions throughout our lifetime. Divorce just happens to be one of the most intense forms.

You can get your life back. You may not be able to save your marriage, but you can discover yourself anew and build a new life based on strength. You can work through this temporary wounding, find restored strength, and create a happy life. You can design your life any way that you like, and as you put in diligent effort to make it come to be, you will have it. You are capable, and you are worth it.

The Turning Points

Recovering from divorce is like walking a labyrinth. At times it doesn't seem to lead anywhere. There are many twists and turns, and any number of dead ends. But eventually it leads you to center.

I've identified five basic turning points through this labyrinth. Each one is different in the way it feels, and what it will require of you. This book series will help you traverse each one to bring you truly beyond divorce. The book you hold will guide you through the first three turning points and whet your appetite for the last two, which will be discussed more fully in a subsequent book.

You will notice that I have arranged these points in a spiral. Spirals are beautifully proportioned, graceful shapes found in nature—in shells, sunflowers, and the spiraling of leaves growing toward the sun. Spirals represent growth from the inside out—from tight in a bud to full bloom. Your journey will also be from inside out, from a constricted place of pain that holds tightly to itself, to the spaciousness of having your feet spread wide and your arms raised high when you are truly *beyond divorce*.

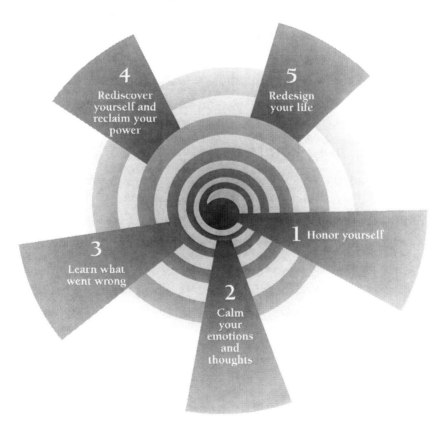

Here are the turning points in summary:

1. Honor yourself: You are going through a difficult life experience. You need to practice extreme self-care. Own the experience as yours. Honor it. Love yourself through it. You need a champion in your corner and it makes sense that it be you, first and foremost. Honoring your process and taking care of yourself is vital, especially in the initial stages.

This first turning point is discussed in the first seven chapters. It is foundational to all the rest.

2. Calm your emotions and thoughts: This is part of honoring yourself. Your emotions and thoughts are working overtime right now. As your internal messengers, they have a lot to say. You won't always understand their message. Be empathetic toward them. Embrace them as if they were a hurting child; they are a part of you.

This is such an important part of your recovery that chapters 8 through 18 are dedicated to this second turning point.

3. Learn what went wrong: Part of calming your emotions and thoughts is understanding what you could have done differently. Emotions and intellect are different. Sometimes, when the mind can understand, the emotions don't have to be quite so loud. There are common reasons that relationships end. Knowing what they are will help you feel more solid and bring you hope.

Chapters 19 through 23 are dedicated to this third turning point.

4. Rediscover yourself and reclaim your power:

The hope you gain from taking care of yourself, calming your emotions and thoughts, and understanding what went wrong, will give you energy to embrace the new possibilities unfolding around you. Discovering yourself anew is an adventure, potent with discoverable desires and passions. Reclaiming your power sets you solidly on the path of creating a new life you love.

Chapters 24 through 26 touch on these topics.

5. Redesign your life:

It is at this turning point that you will take the new you for a test drive. Yep, it's a little scary. Taking charge of our lives is a big deal. But it's also incredibly exciting and full of potential. This is your opportunity to create a future worth having.

Chapters 27 through 31 cover many important aspects of redesigning your life, the fifth turning point.

Points four and five require a lengthy conversation in and of themselves. More of that discussion will come in another book. The first three steps are most important to you right now.

Even though the five turning points are predictable, moving through them is not a linear process as in moving from one to the next; rather, they build on each other like the rings of a tree. In that, the first turning point, "honor yourself," is inherent in all five points. Similarly, the first four turning points are inherent in and necessary to recreating your life, which is point five.

You may loop back through one or several of these turning points more times than you like. I hope you won't become too discouraged when that happens. It's a necessary part of moving *beyond divorce*. I assure you that when you do revisit a turning point it will be with more resources than you had prior, which means it won't be as intense and won't last as long. Think of it as a revisit to tidy up more loose ends.

I will, from time to time throughout the book, alert you to the turning points so you will know which you are traveling through. You will move through them organically, and at your own pace, as a result of working through the chapters.

Where We Are Going

Your destination on this journey *beyond divorce* isn't simply to get things back to normal—to the way things once were. We are going beyond—to a life lived from your highest and best self—to the part of you that is creative, resourceful, and wise. The part that knows abundance, joy, gratitude, calm, presence, goodness, kindness, and the like. Your true self is waiting to be expressed.

The opposite of living from those qualities is living in fear, which is an extension of ego—a false self. Perhaps you recognize that that is where you are even now. Fear reacts instead of acts, is on guard instead of at peace, fears instead of trusts, lashes out instead of speaks from confidence. A major loss cracks open this fearful egoic shell and allows us a glimpse of the creative, peaceful place deep inside, sometimes for the first time in our lives.

Throughout the text I will point you to opportunities to go within and find your calm center, to let go of fear, to trust. There is a peace beneath your circumstances, and we are going to find it.

How We Get There: Practicing Presence

The past and future are both illusions—smoke and mirrors. They do not exist except between our ears. Right now is the only moment in which we can take meaningful action.

> **We can create a lot of pain for ourselves by reliving a past that no longer applies and by projecting either fears or hopes onto a phantom future.**

When we can become present, we are in direct contact with the portal of peace—the portal of healing. Pain and fear don't live there. If you wish to find the peace that is beneath and despite your circumstances, you will want to heed the calls to become present when I discuss them throughout the book. I will refer to them as being with what is, staying present, and present-moment awareness.

Becoming present is a learned skill, and like any new skill we are initially quite clumsy at it. Be gentle with yourself as you learn.

A Journal

Keep your journal handy on this journey. In several places you will be asked to write down your thoughts. Your journal can serve this purpose. Having your notes in one place allows you to review how far you've come, determine the patterns you are repeating, and it can also be your best friend in the middle of the night when you need to talk and the world is asleep.

Marking Your Progress

Another tool—and one to develop—is the habit of noticing exactly where you are on the journey. Throughout this book I have provided "Where Are You Now?" or "How Are You Doing?" scales to help you assess where you are with the current topic. They will provide a quick look at where you are and what you want to work on for your healing and growth. I encourage you to complete each one, marking your position on the scale. You may want to date your marks so you can see your progress when you revisit it at a future time. On some, the progression goes from left to right, the right being the more recovered position. On others the more recovered position is closer to center. The arrows will guide you on those.

Let's start with your first assessment.

Where Are You Now?

At almost any trailhead there is a map marked with an 'X' and the words, "You are here." Before embarking on an unknown trek it is important to orient yourself. You want to know where you are and have at least an idea about where you are going. People come to divorce in a variety of mental states, financial situations, levels of support, and many other variables. We can literally be all over the map.

Look at these descriptors and circle those that fit you.

In Denial   Terrified   Hating It   Devastated/Surviving

One Part of Me Has Moved On—

Other Parts Are Coming to Grips

At Peace with It   Hopeful   Figuring It Out   Stuck

Moving On   Curious About Me   Stuck   Done   Resigned

Kicking and Screaming   Curious

See Light at the End of a Dark Tunnel

Are there any others you would add?

One place is not better or worse than another. Where you are is just right. When you are at peace with where you are, you will see your choices more clearly, allowing you to move on in a meaningful way. It doesn't mean resigning yourself to a bad situation. You're simply acknowledging what is rather than denying it. You can't take action in the past or the future, only right here, right now, with what is.

Part One

GATEWAY TO TRANSFORMATION

Divorce as Opportunity

Just when the caterpillar thought life
was over, it became a butterfly.

A s we begin this journey of healing from the losses of your divorce or significant relationship breakup, I want to give you some hope by pointing out that there is also an opportunity in this experience—even though it may not feel like an opportunity right now. I understand that you are hurting, confused, and afraid. The emotions are intense, and it is easy to feel overwhelmed. Many times it's appropriate to feel overwhelmed. There's a lot going on. But what I want for you is to understand that there is a bigger picture, a positive side, a transformative side, to all that you are going through. Understanding that you are on the threshold of one of life's most transformational events may help make sense of it all. It would be a shame to miss the good in this experience.

You will be different on the other side of your divorce. Just how different will depend on how you approach your recovery. If you can find the courage to examine how you participated in and contributed to the ending of your relationship, and if you are determined to learn from it, you will become more open, loving, and compassionate, and you will experience possibilities beyond what you can see right now. If you aren't willing to change and grow, you will miss this opportunity and divorce will not be as transformational for you. It will be one more deflating experience that leaves you bitter and angry.

Ways Divorce Is an Opportunity

1. Divorce Is a Wake-Up Call

Divorce is one of life's many wake-up calls. It provides a lightbulb moment when, perhaps for the first time, you become fully alert to the state of your life. You see others, and yourself, with new clarity. Most often we don't like what we see at this first clear look, but divorce also provides the opportunity to recreate yourself.

2. Divorce Gives You the Opportunity to Examine Your Life with New Eyes

Most losses in life cause us to examine what is truly important. Divorce is unique in that it touches every aspect of life: mental, emotional, physical, spiritual, family, finances, health, friends, career, future, housing, recreation, other relationships including future romantic interests, and on and on. There is not a single area that divorce won't impact. But the good news is that you get to put it all back together in whatever way suits you. You have before you an opportunity to create more, new, different, and better.

When you clean out the junk drawer at home, you make a keep-or-throw decision on every single item—from the rubberband ball to the gum wrappers to the matchbook from that place that went out of business ten years ago. Divorce will cause you to make those kinds of decisions about your life. What will you keep? What will you throw away? What needs to be returned to its rightful owner or recycled?

3. Divorce Requires You to Let Go of an Outdated Version of Yourself

You will let go as you move through the emotions of grief, anger, sadness, and hurt. You will let go of your damaged self-worth and move into a new and better image of yourself, maybe even catching a glimpse of the you that you've always wanted to be. The opportunity of divorce allows you to proactively design your life and not just settle for the life you've been handed. You can live your "Life by Design," not by default. (Discovering that I could live my life by design and not default led to my using Life by Design as my business name.) Now is your chance.

4. Divorce Helps You Develop Important Life Skills

Through the divorce process you will learn skills that will serve you for the rest of your days. Grieving well is a life skill. So is boundary setting and maturing in anger. Managing your thinking so you can take charge of your own self-worth is a gift that will keep on giving. It takes consistent practice to recognize your feelings and accept responsibility for them, and to learn that you can choose how to respond in each moment.

5. Divorce Helps You Learn from the Past to Create a Different Future

Learning what went wrong in your ended relationship brings some semblance of order to the process. It is no longer some haphazard event that happened to you. When you understand your part, you understand how to create differently in the future. This puts you behind the wheel of your own driver's seat. Divorce allows you to release the past right here in the present, in order to release your future.

6. Divorce Helps You Find the Real You

When Michelangelo was asked how he created such beautiful sculptures, he spoke of the image contained in the stone. He chipped away the encasing stone to release the image inside. Divorce is like that. There is a new and beautiful version of yourself waiting to be released. Every step you take in your divorce—whether it's meeting with your attorney, preparing financial papers, working out a parenting plan, or sharing tears with a friend—brings you one step closer. It all works together. And as hard as it is to believe right now, all the angst is eventually worth it. I have absolute faith that you will come to a positive outcome in your divorce journey. If you can't believe that just yet, I invite you to lean on my faith in you until you can find your own.

You will discover that you are courageous, powerful, and wise far beyond what you have recognized. Your emerging reality will be more workable than the one you leave behind and will allow you to have the peace, happiness, and stability you crave. As you step into this new way of being, you will attract connections and resources that you couldn't imagine before.

Many people are surprised at the lightness and energy they feel after their recovery work. They say that, given the insights and renewed sense of self that they have experienced, divorce was an okay event after all. Why? Certainly not because of what they've lost. Losses are painful even if they eventually bring us to a better place. It's okay because they get in touch with their strengths—often for the first time. The face in the mirror becomes a friend. Life begins to make sense. You can have this sense of renewal, too.

You don't have to live in a world where you use most of your energy just to hold yourself together.

Life has more to offer than that.

In working with this material you are not only recovering from the shock of your ended relationship, you are recovering the truest part of yourself that you lost along the way. This true self is free, boundless, peaceful, joyful, and powerful. It is the sacred part of yourself that you are journeying toward.

Even though there will be times when you cannot find the path, I promise that there is always a next step to take. Take that one. One step at a time is all you need.

Welcome to the journey!

Where Are You Now?

How do you view your divorce?

I see no good in
this divorce.

I can see this as
an opportunity.

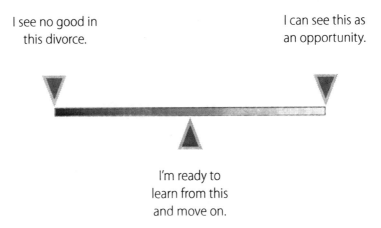

I'm ready to
learn from this
and move on.

2

Living in the In-Between

Difficulties are opportunities to better things,
they are stepping stones to greater experience.
Perhaps some day you will be thankful
for some temporary failure in a particular direction.
When one door closes, another always opens;
as a natural law it has to be, to balance.

—BRIAN ADAMS, *HOW TO SUCCEED*

Have you been shaken to your core? Do you feel your life is scattered in pieces around you? Are you worn out from trying to keep things from falling apart? These are common experiences for those in the middle of a transition. If you've experienced the unpredictable shaking of an earthquake, you're familiar with the In-Between Zone. This is the vulnerable space between what was and what is yet to come. It is the emotional version of a literal earthquake.

Many metaphors have been used to describe the In-Between Zone. One I particularly like is *Star Trek's* transporter. While being transported, the person or item is broken down to molecules, which remain in flux until they are reassembled in a new place, often on an entirely different planet. Especially if you were in a long relationship,

you may have all the feelings of being dumped onto an
alien world. Time is different. The geography is different.
The culture is different. If you're trying to retrain to re-
enter the job market, you may find that the skills that once
served you no longer do. You may wonder how you will
survive.

The only thing certain in the In-Between Zone is
uncertainty—an uncertain outcome, an uncertain identity, an uncertain future. Uncertainty makes us afraid. We
feel anxious when we have so little control. Like a car
floating in a river, we steer like crazy but we are still at
the mercy of the river. It's hard not to worry about what is
around the next corner.

In the In-Between Zone you may feel as though:

* you've been broken apart
* a part of you has died
* your anger is out of proportion
* you experience symptoms of grief
* your memory is less efficient or nonexistent
* you are numb
* you are lost and disoriented, much like a hiker
  lost deep in the woods
* you are vulnerable and scared
* your life is in complete flux
* your drive to find stability becomes all
  consuming

As hard as it is, and as little prepared as we are for such an experience, such an experience, we must learn to embrace the uncertainty as our new reality in order to deal successfully with our situation. When we're okay with not knowing, the situation, to a degree, becomes an adventure instead of a nightmare. We can be curious instead of full of dread. As best you can, take each moment as it comes without piling on regrets of the past or fears of the future. One moment at a time is more manageable.

How Long Does It Last?

There is no formula for predicting how long you will be in the In-Between Zone. It is not as if we can say that for a marriage of fifteen years, you can expect to be in the In-Between Zone for six months or two years. Many factors contribute to its intensity and its length, such as how long you were married, how old you were when you got married, your ability to speak up, your ability to ask for support, your proficiency with daily tasks such as laundry, cooking, and managing car repairs; your financial situation; the number and ages of your children; and many other things. The best answer I have is, it takes as long as it takes. One thing is certain: When you are in it, it seems like an eternity.

Just like the trapeze artist, we must let go of one reality in order to grab another. It's scary because no matter how beautiful we imagine our future to be, it is intangible until we have it in our grasp. Because we like life to be predictable and controllable, it is disconcerting to be with the chaos of the In-Between Zone. The good news is that the very reason it is disconcerting is also the reason it is so powerful and ultimately an agent of change.

The Power of the In-Between Zone

The In-Between Zone is inherently creative precisely *because* it is so tenuous. If you could take the pieces of your life, shake them up, spread them out in front of you, then pick the parts you want to keep, leaving the rest, you would experience the creative power of the In-Between Zone. One man told me that after his divorce he re-examined every piece of his life—whether it was beliefs, behaviors, or friends—for its inherent value to the person he had become. Brick upon brick he rebuilt his life based on the solid foundation of those things purposefully chosen. Imagine creating your life in such a conscious way. Not leaving a single brick to chance, but each one carefully chosen for its unique value.

William Bridges in his book *The Way of Transition* champions the In-Between Zone (which he calls the Neutral Zone) for its creative power in our lives. It is in the in-between that we find doorways to a whole different way of seeing and understanding the world.

The breakdown of our old reality releases the energy that was trapped there and frees it for our use in creating something new.

Learning to *be* with your emotions, letting go of an expected outcome, and surrounding yourself with people who care are the most useful and least painful ways to navigate this transformation.

Identifying the positive outcome of previous transitions in your life can help you see that the In-Between Zone you are experiencing right now will also turn out to be positive.

Set an Intention

Take a moment to identify a few positive things you believe will come from your divorce. For example,

- I will begin to focus on the good that is all around me.
- I will cherish my time with my children.

Chances are you thought of more than two. Having a long list of positive intentions is helpful. Make your list as long as you can and revisit it often.

A New Beginning

All of the turmoil of the In-Between Zone is ultimately leading you to a new and better place. At some point, your emotions will begin to settle down. You will feel alive again, and feel more yourself than you've ever felt before. You may resume hobbies abandoned years ago or take up new ones. You may contact people you've lost touch with. Realizing how much you missed by isolating yourself during your marriage, you swear off that and jump back into life with gusto. Eventually, you will incorporate new world views into your revised map of reality. Things that were previously a source of pain no longer cause suffering. Challenging situations are met with confidence instead of fear. Each of these becomes a key component in the new future that is revealing itself.

In The New Beginning stage you will likely feel:

- stability in all areas of life
- relief that the battle is over
- pride and a sense of accomplishment
- deep gratitude
- acknowledgment of the skills you've learned
- curiosity about what is next

In the New Beginning stage, you will begin to develop a vision for your future. Even though you can't see it right now and you're not supposed to see it right now, your new life is waiting. More importantly, there is a new you emerging who will take you there. You are transforming from the inside out. Changes are already taking place deep within. You may experience them as a disconcerting rumble, but they will lead to stability once again. You will travel through the uncertainty to find solid ground in a life you love.

Where Are You Now?

Look at the stages of transition in the graphic on page 16. Notice the progressive emotions on each side of the In-Between Zone, with the more intense emotions closest to it. Indicate where you are. It's not unusual to experience several emotions at one time.

New Beginning

Enthusiasm • Creativity • Purpose

Hope • Optimism • Control
Risk-taking • Acceptance • Impatience

Skepticism

Broken Fear
Hopeless
Tenuous Tired

In-Between Zone

Edgy Purposeless
Worried
Anxious

Loss of Control

Confusion • Frustration

Anger • Fear • Grief • Shock • Denial

Relationship Ending

Enter here

3

Moving toward Acceptance

Accept — then act.
Whatever the present moment contains,
accept it as if you had chosen it.
Always work with it, not against it.

— ECKHART TOLLE

Accepting that you are divorcing is one of the hardest parts of this experience. If you didn't, or don't, want the divorce, accepting it may be especially difficult. *"Why would I want to accept that my relationship is over when I am completely opposed to it ending?"* That is a great question. You don't have to *want* the divorce in order to accept that it is happening. Acknowledging the truth is the first step to freeing your energy for healing. Accepting allows you to see effective next steps and is prerequisite to letting go. Besides that, resisting reality is exhausting.

Trying to Control the Uncontrollable

Fighting reality is a little like fighting gravity. Reality always wins. Trying to muscle things into alignment with how we believe things should be requires emotional energy that would be better used for other things. I can tell you from experience that it is mentally and physically exhausting to try to control the uncontrollable. Life will not be controlled. Your Ex will not be controlled, the courts will not be controlled, and you will have little energy left for other things, including healing, if you try to exert control over these uncontrollable things.

Children try to control their world, wanting what they want, when they want it. As adults, we realize that the world is uncontrollable and learn to be flexible and move stealthily through the reality in which we find ourselves.

Accepting What Is

Once we realize that we create more pain for ourselves by resisting, the obvious solution is to accept things as they are. This is the first turning point. Honoring yourself means letting yourself off the hook. For you, acceptance may mean coming to grips with the fact that your relationship is ending, that your partner had an affair, or that there is more debt than assets. Acceptance may begin by simply admitting that your partner doesn't love you anymore, or at least doesn't love you enough to work on the relationship. Accepting reality doesn't make you a failure; it doesn't really change anything external. It changes *you*. It puts you in alignment with what is. Acceptance may not come easily or quickly, but it is one of the best things you can do for yourself.

Accepting doesn't mean you just accept what your Ex says about you, or that you accept his or her poor behavior.

Not at all. You don't close your eyes to reality. Instead, you see the situation at face value and make as informed a decision, or take as decisive an action, as possible. You don't allow a lot of thought-time between what is happening and the action you take. If you're finding it difficult to take action, you may be secretly hoping reality will change. This is the opposite of accepting things as they are and taking a stand for yourself. If your Ex is emptying the bank accounts, immediate action is required.

Embracing Resistance

Resistance is an inside job. It is your ego's natural reaction to what it perceives to be an objectionable situation. The ego survives on fear. It will try to gain control by fortifying itself. It believes that by resisting it, what ever "it" is, it will go away.

Here are a few signs you aren't accepting what is:

- finding yourself preoccupied with or obsessing over recurring thoughts about the situation
- being short-tempered and impatient, easily frustrated, and tense
- feeling angry that things aren't going your way or that the other person doesn't see things your way.

We often keep painful conversations or events alive through our own compulsive thinking. Have you ever found yourself fuming over a situation that happened last week,

last month, or even last year? A lot of the pain we experience is due to our own thinking. In Part 4: Managing Your
Thoughts, you will learn techniques to get to the peace that
is beneath those painful thoughts. Managing your thinking
and calming your emotions are the two prongs of the second
turning point.

Exercises for Releasing Resistance

Here are some tips for releasing your resistance when
you're ready. Resistance can shield us from things we're
not yet able to deal with, which is a good thing, but there
will come a time that you must embrace rather than resist
in order to move on. Practice any or all of these as often
as you need to.

You may want to replace the word *resistance* with
something that is real for you. Perhaps, "I'm getting
divorced" or "I'm losing my 401K" or "My partner doesn't
love me anymore." I will use the example "I'm getting
divorced" to illustrate.

- **Use your mind.** Pay attention to when, and
  under what conditions, the thought "I'm getting
  divorced" shows up. Observe your response.
  Don't judge, analyze, or be self-critical. Just
  watch. Just by observing, you have created
  distance between you and the thought, which
  makes room for a different perspective.

- **Use your body.** The resistance is *in* you. Sit
  down, relax as best you can, take a few deep,
  slow breaths. When you feel relaxed, do a head-
  to-toe body scan. Feel into places resistance may

be hiding. Where in your body do you feel it? Do you feel it as a knot in your stomach? Tightness in your throat? Tenseness down the back of your legs? Tears welling up? Once you've found it, take several minutes to direct your breath deeply into that place where the resistance resides. Feel that area open and expand as the knot of resistance releases. You may feel a powerful emotion. Often, there is a clarifying perspective that comes forth when the area releases, as if something had been trapped there.

- **Use your imagination.** Feel the resistance as if it were a cloak or a jacket around your shoulders. Feel the tightness of its confining nature. When you have a good sense of it, imagine shrugging it off and onto the floor. Pause for a minute to notice how it feels to drop the weight of it. Do you sense more possibilities with the weight of resistance off your shoulders?

- **Use your heart.** In your mind's eye, picture yourself answering your front door to see Resistance standing there. What does it look like? Is it wrinkly and knotty? Is it The Hulk? Is it a rope or other restraining device? What does it want? Instead of slamming the door, draw it in. Smile, offer it tea, befriend it. Make it welcome. Have a chat. Often, when we welcome resistance in this way we find it has an important message for us. That message may very well be that all-important next step you're seeking.

- **Use it to practice being present.** When you notice yourself upset by something out of your control like a cancelled appointment, or your Ex letting you know s/he can't pick up the kids from school, say out loud, "I accept this change." Say it until you feel a shift from the shock of learning about it to acceptance and action.

In time, you will embrace all of your journey, not just the parts that were initially appealing like being on your own or away from someone who treated you poorly. There is necessary growth and useful insights during each part of the process. Even though you want things to go quickly there are important things to tend to all along this path; proceeding slowly will allow you the time to tend to them with care. It would be a shame to go through all this and miss the benefits.

Where Are You Now?

Where are you on the resistance scale?

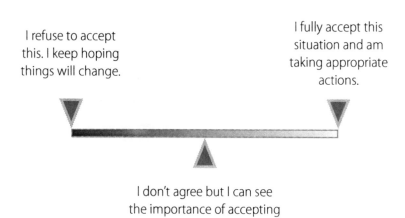

I refuse to accept this. I keep hoping things will change.

I fully accept this situation and am taking appropriate actions.

I don't agree but I can see the importance of accepting things as they are.

Part Two

ALONE AGAIN

Surviving Survival Mode

*Ever has it been that love knows not its own depth
until the hour of separation.*

— KAHLIL GIBRAN

In the earliest stages of divorce, when you feel overwhelmed, it may be difficult to think clearly, make decisions, or remember even the simplest things. You might find yourself turning right instead of left out of your driveway to get to the grocery store you've been to a hundred times. You may feel like you're lost, overwhelmed, can't quit crying, can't think straight; you may have panic attacks or cocoon. In this chapter we will practice skills to help you transition out of a survival state and into stability.

Skills for Surviving

As I read the book *Deep Survival: Who Lives, Who Dies, and Why* by Laurence Gonzales, I was struck by how closely the capacities needed to survive in natural catastrophes apply to divorce. He says that people who have not had to struggle in their lives are in more peril when faced with a catastrophe than those who have had previous struggles.

In essence, practice helps. If this is your first major loss, and divorce often is, it can easily overwhelm your inner resources.

"All survivors I've talked to have told me how horrible the experience was," says Gonzales. "But they have also told me, often with deep puzzlement, how beautiful it was. They wouldn't trade the experience for anything in the world."[1] It is my experience that most divorce survivors—eventually—feel the same way. Whether lost in the natural wilderness or the mental wilderness of a world turned upside-down, we are stripped of security, thrown into a survival state, and we are forced to find something much deeper in ourselves to rely on. And we have access to that something deeper for the rest of our lives.

Gonzales found that common to all survivors is their ability to take personal responsibility and not blame anyone or anything for their dilemma. That will help you, too.

Suggestions for Surviving

Gonzales studied the thoughts and behaviors common to wilderness survivors. I have reframed them below as suggestions to help you survive when you are disoriented by your breakup and your sense of stability is most fleeting. Notice the parallels between wilderness survival and your own situation.

- Remain calm. Do not panic. Maintain control of your emotions.

- Allow yourself only one thought: What is my next correct action?

- Use any fear you have as sustenance. Let the energy feed action.

- Proceed with great caution if the next step requires great risk.

- Pace yourself. Rest often. Pushing too hard can cause emotional, mental, and physical fatigue that will require weeks or months of recovery.

- Make a plan for the immediate future. Trying to plan too far ahead may elicit unwanted emotions. Survivors set small, manageable goals and systematically go about achieving them.

- Do the best you can. Anything less than that will not get you through.

- Know that you cannot change the world; you can only change yourself. Accept the reality in which you find yourself. Calm yourself and begin taking action.

- Hold to a vision of what you want, what you have to live for. Use your imagination to create a compelling future that will draw you through.

- Delight in small achievements and celebrate simple victories as they happen.

- Look within yourself, not to your circumstances, for balance.

- Pray. (Gonzales found survivors pray even when they don't believe in a god.) Faith is an important part of one's will to survive.

> ■ Help other survivors. Helping someone else is
> the best way to ensure your own survival. It takes
> you out of yourself and helps you rise above your
> fears.

It may help to decide now which of these suggestions are most useful to you and implement them right away.

Coping Strategies

While we are in a survival state we resort to behaviors that have worked in the past, often behaviors learned in childhood. We hang on to them because we don't know what else to do. These become our coping strategies. Some are good and healthy like going to the gym more often, but sometimes the things we've chosen do more harm than good, like chemical or substance abuse. We believe they will bring comfort or protect us in some way, or sometimes we just want to forget, to take a break from the persistent pain.

If we use our coping strategies to deny reality it only serves to delay positive movement. Here are some of the most common harmful strategies:

■ Compulsive dating, serial sex partners, or
   reliance on pornography in an effort to
   avoid the feelings that come with loss of
   love.

■ Isolating or drinking when depressed
   instead of reaching out to friends.

- Gambling in an attempt to cure financial malaise rather than investing in known returns.

- Overeating or choosing comfort foods that may be unhealthy.

- Overspending, undermining your security.

These strategies may help us cope for a while, but they don't solve anything in the long run. They are temporary band-aids that are ultimately self-defeating. They can take on a life of their own, leaving you with both the original problem, such as financial hardship, and layering on another problem, such as an addiction.

One thing I want you to avoid is "white-knuckling it" and calling that stability. Hanging on tightly to things that do not work in an effort to maintain a sense of calm is not real stability.

Identify Your Coping Strategies

First, think of things you have been doing since your breakup that could be ways of coping with your distress. Next, identify the costs or benefits involved for each one. By "costs," I don't necessarily mean monetary, but costs to your health, your family and other relationships, your work, or your future. Benefits can be things like renewed energy, new friends, or a hobby that enlivens you. Some strategies may have both a cost and a benefit; for example excessive alcohol is obviously harmful to health, but moderate consumption can calm frayed nerves after an intense day. How is your chosen activity helping you, and how might it be hurting you? What healthier choices could you make?

Where Are You Now?

Where are you on the survival scale?

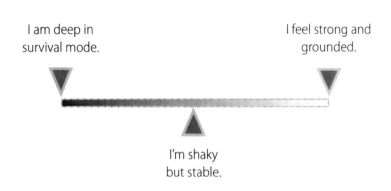

I am deep in survival mode.

I feel strong and grounded.

I'm shaky but stable.

Getting Help

Through humor, you can soften some
of the worst blows that life delivers.
And once you find laughter,
no matter how painful your situation might be,
you can survive it.

— BILL COSBY

It's unfair but true that when we are our least resourceful selves we are required to make some of the most important decisions of our lives. When someone dies there are also many decisions to be made, which is why loved ones gather to help the bereaved. When your relationship dies you need just as much support, perhaps more.

As a nation we tend toward the stoic, but when we're hurting that just doesn't make sense. There is so much to think about, so many emotions to work through, and so much to learn. We need people to talk to so we can bring out our inner turmoil, examine it, and receive much-needed support.

You will want many people in your support community, and you will need to select them carefully. Your attorney may be the most available person with whom to vent, but that is an expensive choice. Attorneys are not trained to deal with the emotional aspects of divorce. You will save yourself a lot of money and get more effective help by finding other outlets for processing your emotions.

Perhaps your own family is a prominent part of your support system. But even the most supportive family can tire of your stories, and sometimes they are so invested in your wellness that they push you along too fast. Many times they hurt also and may provide well-meaning but unknowledgeable input. They may idealize you and demonize your former partner instead of giving you balanced input. At the other extreme, they may take the side of the Ex, rather than yours, creating a double loss.

Your support system can include friends, but if your friends have not been through a divorce they may not be able to relate to the depth of your need. They may be very willing to help, but there will be a limit to their ability to understand what you are going through.

You may be tempted to reach out to your former (or soon to be former) spouse for support. After all, this is the person you have leaned on in the past. Unfortunately, it is a rare situation when two divorcing parties can be supportive of one another while going through the divorce process. Some couples can reconfigure, be supportive, and even develop a friendship afterward, but not in the midst of the divorce.

Ideas for Support

A therapist or coach can help you one on one. A therapist for processing, a coach for moving forward, a systems coach for understanding dynamics. You can do a lot of emotional healing that way. However, I have found that your most effective support system is to be with other people who are going through the same experiences that you are, preferably in a group setting. If you can find a group near you, that will be your most effective option. Check the Beyond Divorce (www.beyonddivorce.com) website for resources near you.

One of the most important uses for your support community is what has been called a "support sandwich" or "bookending." The idea is to sandwich a difficult situation (like attending your child's school event or a friend's wedding when your Ex will be there) between supportive interactions. Talk with your supportive person before the event to be reminded of your strengths, get clear on how you want to be (curious, powerful and assertive, compassionate, or a listener), and set your intentions. After the event you can talk with the same friend again, or with another, to discuss what went well, what you would do differently, and to plan your next steps.

Your support system can include more than just individuals; it can include activities such as a workout, massage, or a meeting with your book club. You will come to appreciate and anticipate the relief and rest in these scheduled events.

What meaningful events can you schedule for yourself?

Identifying Emotional Supporters

- List your supporters. These could include friends, family, a coach, a therapist, church associates, etc. Because schedules are busy and availability can be limited, it is a good idea to have many people on your list. Include phone numbers for easy reference. List them in order of accessibility.

- Circle three people on your list who you can call in an emergency or in the middle of the night when you can't sleep.

- Note three supporters with whom you can share your successes. These can be the same three, or different ones.

Getting Support for Practical Tasks

Many times your partner handled tasks that you weren't much good at, and now you are left to figure them out. How will you balance the checkbook, fix your computer, do laundry, or manage as a single parent? Perhaps a neighbor can teach you how to do your laundry. Maybe your aunt can help you balance your checkbook. Just about any child over age eight can help with computer tasks. There are many needs that are simple to fill with the help of the people already in our lives. An example is a new single dad needing to learn how to braid his daughter's hair. Most women would be glad to help with that if asked.

For help with big tasks like yard cleanup, painting, or moving, invite a group of friends over. Some things are more fun when shared, and they get done faster, too. Buy a few pizzas and a six-pack or iced tea, and make it an event. Anything done with friends helps ease the loneliness common to newly divorced people.

For special situations, you may need to hire help; for example with finding employment, making house repairs, or coaching you through the divorce experience.

Identifying Practical Supporters

Make a list of life areas in which you may need support; include the names of people who could help you now or in the future. Include phone numbers for quick reference. Here are a few suggestions:

- Financial/budgeting/paying bills
- Discussing legal options
- Parenting/kids
- Organizing/scheduling
- Health/fitness/exercise/life balance
- Technical (gadgetry, computer)
- Maintenance of vehicles and home
- Moving, downsizing, revamping property

Reaching Out to Your Supporters

Now that you have identified your supporters, be sure to reach out to them. You might want to put them on alert. You will get through your divorce faster and with less personal injury if you lean on your supporters. It's hard to ask for help, and many of us don't feel very good at it. Often asking for support is the first growth step we face in creating our new life. One of our biggest concerns is being a burden to others.

Tips for Reaching Out

- Discuss things ahead of time. "I'm going through a rough time right now and I will need some people I can call on. Would you be one of those people?"

- Respect requests. Find out who is available when and respect the time boundaries that have been offered you. If they ask you not to phone after 11:00 at night, be sure to honor that.

- Respect immediate boundaries. If something comes up and the person you are talking with has to get off the phone, let them. Don't drag it out for another ten minutes. Call another person on your list if you need additional support.

- Keep the lines of communication open. You might occasionally ask, "Is this too much?" "Are you okay if I share some more?" If you are more extroverted, be aware that you can talk a blue streak and not let others get a word in edgewise. You might identify a signal beforehand so that your listener can flag you if feeling overwhelmed.

- Let your supporters know you are grateful for their time.

- Ask about their needs also, and really listen to them. This will help others feel valued.

Awkward Moments

As skillful as you may be at calling on your support system, there will be times when you have to be on your own in the presence of your former partner, a difficult friend, the judge, or the Ex's new boyfriend or girlfriend. There are a few things you can do to prepare.

Preparing for Awkward Moments

- Utilize the "support sandwich." Set intentions, find your most powerful self (your calm center) and then have the meeting. Afterward call your support person to vent and talk about what you learned or want to do different next time.

- If possible, invite a friend to go with you. People are generally better behaved when there is a third party present, and you will feel supported having someone who cares about you by your side.

- Don't risk more than you can afford to lose. Take appropriate steps to protect your vulnerability as you continue to heal and grow. As your emotional range grows, your vulnerability will begin to be an asset and a strength. Protect yourself, if possible, until you are strong enough to face difficult situations on your own.

- Be gentle with yourself. There is no need to beat yourself up for being anxious, afraid, or angry. Doing so only adds to an already difficult situation. Remember, beating yourself up is something you do to yourself, and you can stop that at any time.

Where Are You Now?

Rate your support system.

I don't need a
support system.
I can handle this
on my own.

I have a strong
support system
and use it often.

I see the importance
of a support
system and am
working on that.

6

Taking Care of You

Transformation is not five minutes from now; it's a present activity. In this moment you can make a different choice, and it's these small choices and successes that build up over time to help cultivate a healthy self-image and self-esteem.

— JILLIAN MICHAELS

A t a poignant time in my journey I heard Dr. Phil say, "You are a life manager and you have one client, which is *you*." I realized that if I had hired someone to run my life the way I'd been doing it, I would have fired her in a minute. I was doing a lousy job. I demanded far more of myself than I was capable of delivering. I was not giving myself time to rest or to eat well. I worried incessantly—as if the more I worried, the better chance I had of things going well. Looking back I know how ridiculous it was, but at the time I was in survival mode. I found that when somebody else (a friend, a book, or even my mother) gave me permission, I could give myself a break, but, somehow, I couldn't do that for myself. If you need someone to give you permission to take it a little easier and practice good self-care, I will be that person.

You must take care of yourself. Taking care of yourself is an integral part of honoring yourself and your process— the first turning point. You are the only person who is with you all the time and who is aware of all that you are juggling and coping with. Only you are keenly aware of the toll the stress is taking on you. You must be the one to put yourself at the top of your priority list. After all, it is your list. What number on your list are you at this moment? Ten? Twenty? Are you even on it?

For many of us, self-care is a huge unknown. Going through a breakup or divorce is a time to take extreme care of yourself. Yes, over-the-top, completely indulgent self-care. It isn't selfish; it is wise. A person hit by a truck doesn't expect to meet the same demands as before they were hit, and you shouldn't either.

The Basics of Self-Care Start with Your Body

Your body bears the brunt of your emotional turmoil, so you must support it. When the body is depleted, you can't think well or make good decisions. Do you take on an excessive schedule, stay up late, or sleep poorly? Do you push yourself with caffeine and neglect taking time for a good meal? When you are exhausted, you tap out your adrenal glands and you have less emotional reserve. Eating well, getting enough sleep, staying hydrated, receiving bodywork (massage or other forms), and exercise are all necessary elements to good self-care—yes, even now when you don't think you can fit one more thing into your schedule. The nervous system and emotions are linked. Caring for one supports the other.

Many of us haven't had to practice extreme self-care, so here are a few suggestions to help out.

Nutrition

Nutrition can achieve results that may be unachievable through any other means. For example, a combination of B vitamins and adequate protein intake can help to stabilize blood sugar, which may also lead to a consistent energy level throughout the day, without the peaks and valleys that a stimulant-based lifestyle can produce. B vitamins and amino acids (protein) can help to improve the emotional state as well, and when combined with the appropriate minerals, including calcium and magnesium, may help you to sleep peacefully throughout the night. Nutritional yeast is an excellent source of food-based B vitamins, and leafy green vegetables (in salads or juiced) are a fine source of minerals.[2]

Your nutritional stress plan should be continued for at least three to six months following the highest level of stress. If after that you still feel like your body is exhibiting signs of depletion or ill-health, it would be good to have an examination and adrenal stress test (via saliva samples) performed by your natural healthcare provider so your individual needs can be addressed.[3]

Alternative therapies such as acupuncture or any of the "energy medicine" therapies including those relying on the meridian system can also provide support for coming back to balance. Acupuncture is a quick way to balance the flow of vital energy throughout the body.[4]

We live in a time when many options for wellness care are readily available. You might experiment to find what works best for you.

Natural Remedies

Natural remedies are very helpful when going through a divorce or any high-stress event. Spending extended time in "fight or flight" or "fright" (frozen) modes necessarily draws down our energy reserves. There may be times you feel full of energy (sometimes too much), and then afterward fall flat with fatigue.

It is a good idea to nurture your body before symptoms make themselves known. It is also wise to avoid depressants such as alcohol or excessive ways of numbing the pain.

Natural Remedies at a Glance[5]

- An extra boost of B vitamins, vitamin C, and vitamin D_3 can keep the body resilient and prevent an energy crash.
- Magnesium is a relaxing mineral that can be ingested (although high doses can cause diarrhea in some people). A warm bath with magnesium

---

crystals and a few drops of lavender oil can bring a tense body back toward neutral and make possible a good night's rest.

- Rescue Remedy, a mixture of Bach Flower remedies found at any health food store, almost magically brings one back to center.

- Adaptogenic herbs, those that help the body adapt to stress, can also be helpful. Common herbs with this therapeutic value are Siberian ginseng, ashwaganda, holy basil, and licorice root. These can be taken in capsule or tincture form, but a warm cup of tea (there are numerous herbal stress-reduction teas) will make you take the time to sit back, breathe, count your blessings, and soothe your soul.

As with any herbs used for medicinal purposes, there can be contraindications with other medications you might be taking, so check on those.

Protecting Your Teeth

In times of stress, you may clench your jaws more than usual and that can carry over to nighttime teeth grinding. A dentist can provide you with a mouth orthotic also known as a splint, which will also support your jaws and your neck, or there are simpler and less expensive store-bought devices to use at night. This tense period won't last forever, but many people find it helpful to protect their teeth and jaws during this stressful time.

Journal Writing

Journal writing can be a useful outlet for self-support. You may not want to wake dear friends at 3:00 a.m. when your thoughts and emotions are overwhelming you. Your journal can be a trusted friend that is always present and willing to listen. You can scream, cry, and cuss in your journal. You can CAPITALIZE and **write in bold,** and use lots of exclamation marks!!!!! You can stab it, pound on it, and scribble on it. You can write in the margins and with different colors and swirls. You can keep it private or you can share it. You can frame it or you can burn it. It will be a record of your journey. If you keep it, you can review it years later to see how far you've come or notice that you're still dealing with some of the same things. It's yours to do with as you wish.

Tips for Enjoying Your Journal

- The most important thing to remember about journal writing is not to box yourself in with rules about how and when to write. If you feel like writing in the morning, then write in the morning. Or at night, write then. If you don't have anything to say, you don't have to write. It is at your service, not the other way around.

- Another important guideline is to make sure your journal stays private, unless you are choosing to share it. If you are concerned about someone else reading it, you won't feel free to be fully honest. If this means putting it under lock and key, do so.

It may be that you can simply speak to the people you live with and explain about the importance of privacy. Because the journal is holding the depth of you, in all your vulnerability, treat it as sacred space.

- Safety is obviously important, and we must feel safe both from others' judgments (which is where privacy comes in) and our own judgments. We must hold our experiences in a compassionate, accepting way to make full use of a journal. This is good practice in any area of our life, at any time.

Collage or Visual Journal

An alternative to the written journal is to cut out images from magazines or other sources, including your own photos. A collage reveals internal realities of which you may be unaware. The most useful time for a visual journal is when your emotions are all tied up in knots and you are helpless to sort them out. It can be very revealing to choose a number of visual images. You may respond with *"Oh, that's what this is about"* when you see a representative picture.

Making a Collage or Visual Journal

- Choose several magazines with topics or activities that are interesting to you. These can be magazines related to hobbies, sports, children, or other interests. They need to be human-based, not technology-type manuals.

- Look through the magazines and be aware of the images and words that hook you or catch your attention emotionally in some way. This isn't about what you *think* about them. Focus on what you *feel* about them. Choose words and/or images that provoke an emotional response.

- If you like, you can glue the images on poster board. If you don't feel that creative, that's okay. Just selecting the images serves its own purpose. If you like what you create, you might want to have it laminated.

Using your collage:

✓ Do some journaling around the images that you have chosen. What do you notice? What do the images reveal about you and to you? Pay special attention to the values revealed. Allow yourself to be surprised by what you see when looking at the collage as one piece.

✓ Talk to a friend, therapist, or your coach about your creation, asking the same questions as above.

✓ Put your collage in a prominent place in your home where you will see it and be reminded by it frequently. Pay attention to it. What is it revealing to you? Note those things in your journal.

Nature

Being in nature, whether a ten-mile hike, a leisurely walk with a friend, or just sitting outdoors, will calm your nerves and bring healing to your soul. Wild places are your friend. Water is especially calming. The bright light the outdoors can lift the blues. Visit places you've never been before. The mind appreciates seeing new things. Many people have found that walking among the trees in a breeze cleanses the palate of the soul.

Music

Music provides another important emotional release and support. I so appreciated songs that spoke to me about what I was going through. John Denver's *Looking for Space* spoke loudly to me because I was almost desperately seeking to find myself. Celine Dion singing *My Heart Will Go On* was another good one when my heart was breaking. One woman listened to Yanni's *In the Mirror* album any time she wanted consolation. Low-key instrumental music and meditative CDs are also good, as are recordings of nature sounds such as wind, rain, and waterfalls. Find what works for you. Put them on your iPod or make a CD that is accessible to you when you need it.

Meditation

Meditation, prayer, focused breathing, or any spiritual practice that is meaningful to you will serve to center and ground you. Sitting quietly while focusing on your breath or your center can help you access your inner calm. That calm is always in there somewhere; it's just that life is too noisy to be able to access it. Sitting quietly helps you find it.

Prayer will help you feel undergirded by something larger than yourself. You won't find inner calm in do-ing; you will find it by be-ing still, and sometimes we need to feel held in order to relax into stillness. If this is a new practice for you there are many guides to help. I will also remind you to become present at key times throughout this book.

Which of these ideas for self-care do you want to adopt? Are there others you would add?

Where Are You Now?

Where are you on the self-care scale?

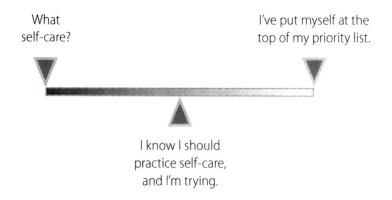

What self-care?

I've put myself at the top of my priority list.

I know I should practice self-care, and I'm trying.

The Impact of Divorce

Divorce is like two lions in a den attacking each other.
You know somebody is going to get hurt real bad.
All kids can do is sit behind a window
and watch it happen.

— NINE-YEAR-OLD BOY, *WWW.DIVORCEANDKIDS.COM*

One of the reasons divorce is so difficult is that it impacts so many different areas of life. You may no sooner get your financial papers completed when you find out you have to sell your home—and moving becomes your next priority. Often there are several areas demanding your attention at the same time. This creates tremendous stress. You can see why it is so important to take good care of yourself and allow others to support you. There is so much going on inside you that it's hard to sort through the demands to determine a single most important thing on which to focus.

To help you determine where specific help will be useful, and to identify things that *are* working, I've devised a simple assessment.

Mapping the Impact of Divorce

Below is a sample figure showing major life areas often impacted by divorce. After reviewing the sample and simple directions, you will complete one of your own.

Generally, the above-the-centerline areas are directly impacted by your divorce—these are things to be done. The items below the centerline are more indirectly impacted as they are supportive of the process.

In many cases one area in disarray impacts several other areas. For example, if the stress of divorce affects your health, you won't be as effective as a parent, at your job, or maintaining your living space.

Below the assessment are a few questions to help you get the most from the exercise. Most people are surprised

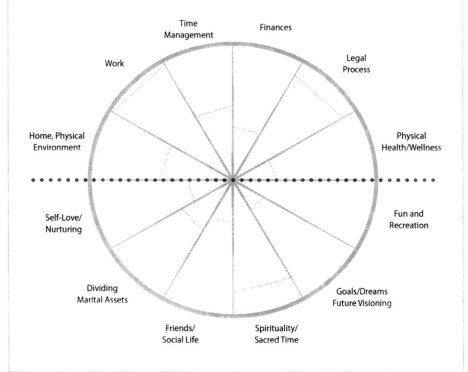

to discover a number of things that *are* working in their lives. That's good to know, too.

The following example shows the results for a male in the early stages of his divorce. Start at 1:00 (Finances) on the chart and proceed clockwise.

- Divorce is putting a strain on his earning capacity. His wife worked only part-time because she stayed home with the kids. He was the main provider. He rated "finances" at a 4.

- The legal process for he and his wife has just begun, so for now it is at a 9. (Note: As the divorce progresses his level of functioning in that area could easily drop. This is not quantitative, but about the qualitative: How well are you functioning in this area given your needs?)

- Although he's adamant about working out and tries to eat well, the strain of the divorce is taking its toll on him physically. He rates his "physical health/wellness" at about 4.

- "Fun and recreation" don't even exist. It's at a 0.

- The future feels very chaotic right now, so he's rated goals, dreams, and future visioning at a 2.

- His spiritual practice is very important to him. He tries not to let anything get in the way of that. He rates "spirituality/sacred time" at about an 8.

- He believes that he will get around to spending time with his friends when everything settles down. For now, he rates "friends/social life" at about 3.

- "Dividing marital assets" is proving to be more difficult than he thought. He rated that area at about 3.

- He tends to be hard driving and doesn't cut himself much slack. He rates "self-nurturing" at a 2.

- He is moving out of the family home so his children and their mother will have a stable place to live. He rates "home/physical environment" at about 3.

- He has a steady job, so he rated "work" at a 10.

- He's pretty good at managing his time; there just doesn't seem to be enough of it. He's rated his functioning level of "time management" about 5.

Now it's your turn. Rate your approximate level of functioning in the life areas represented. It doesn't have to be exact. Please don't get stuck on the numbers themselves. Remember that this is about *your* experience. Your former mate would likely complete it differently. It doesn't matter what s/he would do, mark what is true for you. You can do this assessment many times as things change during your divorce. If you think you'll want to do this assessment more than once, you may want to copy it first. Noting the date you complete it may also be useful.

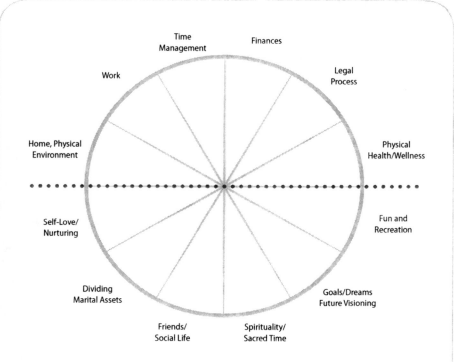

Getting the Most from Your Chart

After you've completed your chart, spend some time with these questions. It is important to notice the things you are doing well and to acknowledge the ways you can carry that strength into other areas that need assistance.

- In which life area are things going well?
- List three things that you are *already doing* that are having a positive impact on your situation.
- Into which area could you interject change in order to cause the greatest shift in all areas?
- What is one thing that you can do this week to begin that shift?

Now that you know the importance of self-care, allowing yourself to be supported, and on which areas you would like to focus, let's turn to calming your emotions.

Part Three

RESOLVING THE EMOTIONS

8

Working with Feelings

If I'd never met you, I wouldn't like you.
If I didn't like you, I wouldn't love you.
If I didn't love you, I wouldn't miss you.
But I did, I do, and I will.

— Author Unknown

I f this is your first major loss, and divorce often is, the intensity of the emotions may take you by surprise. There isn't much in life that prepares us for the divorce journey.

Many people think only of the legal aspects when considering divorce. How hard can that be? You file the papers, wait the allotted time, the judge signs the final orders, and you're done, right? Sort of. It may seem like a legal process with some emotional components, but in actuality, divorce is much more an emotional experience with some legal aspects to it.

The Powerful Emotions of Divorce

Grief and anger are two powerful emotions present throughout the divorce process. They will show up intermittently throughout. In the beginning, one or the other will be stronger. Thankfully, they don't show up with equal intensity at the same time. Working through the emotions to a healthy completion is the focus of the second turning point. Working through them means both embracing them and resolving them. In the process, the emotions also need to mature. Fortunately, in their mature forms the feelings aren't as painful.

Woven in and around anger and grief, depending on circumstances, are other major emotions such as loneliness, guilt, rejection, anxiety, shame, and fear, making for a difficult emotional soup. Working through these emotions brings relief. It can also bring discouragement when you find yourself looping back through emotions you thought you'd left behind. There is a dance or orchestration between emotions as healing takes place. It is not a linear process.

Ultimately, in order to move on with our lives, we need to disengage from our former partner and our former life. Our emotions are both our guides and our gauge as to how we're doing at this. We can't handle experiencing all of the emotions at one time, so our psyche chooses the strongest emotion in any given moment to concentrate on. When that emotion is at a manageable level, it will move on to the next one that needs attention. They play off of each other throughout the divorce process, intensifying and calming as you work through them or as situations change. Honor yourself as you turn your attention inward—your emotions need your attention now. This is where the second turning point, calm your emotions and thoughts, begins to build on the first turning point, self-care. It is deep internal work and will require some self-focus. You will honor yourself by acknowledging that it is a necessary part of your process. It is not selfish to take care of yourself.

Anger, grief, your self-worth, and how much you've disengaged from your former partner are all linked together. Like the Whac-A-Mole game at Chuck E. Cheese restaurants, you just get one emotion to go below and another pops up somewhere else.

- If your self-worth has taken a hit, you may not feel confident enough to express your anger. As your self-worth improves, you will begin to express your anger and stand up for yourself. Anger provides the needed momentum to set limits.

- As your anger begins to resolve, you will start to feel the sadness that your anger shielded you from. In your sadness you realize you haven't let go as much as you thought you had.

- Working through your grief helps you to let go a little more, which allows you to feel a stronger sense of self.

- This stronger sense of self may loop back to denied and possibly disguised anger feelings. "I'm moving on. I don't care what the SOB does any more." That angry charge alerts you that you are still connected on at least one of three levels that we will talk about later, and more letting go is needed.

You may feel discouraged as you think of revisiting these stages more than once. I assure you that each time you loop through they will resolve more quickly and the feelings will be less intense, leading to an ultimate resolve.

By being present with the emotions as they arise, the intensity will eventually lessen. Between their cycles you are able to gather insights and resources with which to better address them the next time they appear. Being present with emotions means embracing your feelings. If you are sad, allow the sadness. If you are angry, honor that. Denying what you feel, or muscling through difficult situations, will take its toll in the form of physical illness or unexpected emotional outbursts. Embracing your emotions will help you to pass through them more easily. We will talk about the importance of including other people in this process shortly.

You will experience different emotions depending on whether you initiated the divorce or were on the receiving end of that decision.

If Your Partner Initiated the Divorce: You Are the Heartbroken

The person on the receiving end of the divorce decision takes the hardest emotional hit. You've had no time to prepare. It's like being hit by a train. This type of loss is sudden. It is traumatic. You may feel as though you are hanging on by your fingernails. You've been tossed without warning into the ambiguity of the In-Between Zone.

It is very important for you to take care of yourself, especially while you are in this state of shock. You may try to carry on with daily life as you always have, although in my opinion, it's simply not possible. As the Heartbroken, you are in emotional ICU. Remember the cartoon of the guy wrapped head to toe in bandages, leg in a sling, with only a slit for his eyes? That's you. You can't see the bruises on the emotional body, but they are there nonetheless. You might be surprised at the intensity of your feelings and believe that no one else has ever hurt as badly. We humans are good at hiding our emotions. We don't see people around town or at work bursting into tears. I assure you, you are not the only one who feels this way. It is normal for this experience. If your partner is hell-bent on divorcing it's time to take care of yourself and move on.

If your partner wants to move quickly, there may be very little time for you to adjust to the wave of emotions before the legal divorce begins. This means that the intense emotional processing must be done during and after the legal divorce process. Your partner may find completion in the finality of the divorce, while you are still spinning. As much as you can, require things to slow down. Give yourself time to think. You have more influence than you realize.

It often looks to the Heartbroken as if their partner has moved on and is happy in his or her new life. That is not true in the majority of divorces. It's just that the emotions are different. The Heartbreaker is also having his or her own difficult experience that we'll talk about next.

The predominant emotions for the Heartbroken are fear and rejection. We will talk about both and provide some ways to relieve them in the next few chapters. The good news is that the pain usually drives the Heartbroken to seek help, which makes the recovery faster, easier, and more effective than for those who try to muscle through on their own.

If You Initiated the Divorce: You Are the Heartbreaker

For the person initiating the divorce, whom I am calling the Heartbreaker, the emotional separation began somewhere between months and years before any papers were filed. You were probably discontented with your marriage for quite some time. Maybe you stuck it out for the sake of the children, or out of guilt, a sense of duty, or the agreements you made with yourself about commitment and what it means to be married. You may not have even been aware that your discontent would eventually lead to divorce but instead were seeking a little breathing room and are surprised that it's come to this. Unlike the Heartbroken, you have had time to prepare. You have been able to think about the impact to your future, to plan financially, to think about how it might affect the children, to do a fair amount of completion work before ever stating your desire to divorce.

As the Heartbreaker, your feelings around this loss are similar of losing someone to a long-term illness. You've known the end was coming; you just weren't sure when.

Maybe you've thought it through and are just "done." Even though you just want your relationship to be over, it may not be in your best interest to push hard to make it happen quickly. Divorce can only proceed as fast as the slowest partner, and pushing to speed things up can backfire. It is in your best interest to work with, rather than against, your partner's adjustment process.

Moving too quickly also makes it difficult for you to consider all your options. Reconciliation, of course, is one of those options. It is still the best way to avoid divorce pain for you and your kids, and many people consider reconciling when the pain doesn't let up. You might want to keep your heart open, even if it is just a little, until you know that you know, that divorcing is your only option. It may bring you some peace later on to be assured that you did your best with regard to your marriage. It is a painful realization that it takes two to make or heal a relationship, and only one person to end one.

Heartbreakers are often insensitive in the way they announce their desire to divorce. I encourage you to consider the impact your announcement will have on the entire process, on your soon-to-be Ex, your children, and even your extended families and larger community. Choose your words and timing carefully. Avoid making your announcement on important holidays, an anniversary, birthday, or when your spouse is experiencing other major losses, including job loss or health issues.

The predominant emotions for the Heartbreaker are anger, guilt, and sadness, which we will also discuss further.

If You Came to a Mutual Agreement to Divorce

There are couples who mutually agree to divorce. This is often after several attempts to fix the broken relationship, to no avail. After calling it quits and coming back together several times, one person will call for an end to the continual conflict. The partners in these situations may resign themselves because they don't know what else to do. *They think something like: It isn't working, and it apparently is not going to work. I don't want to do this anymore.*

I've never seen two people come to the same decision at exactly the same time. It may happen, but I've not seen it. This means that many couples will go back and forth between the emotions of the Heartbreaker and Heartbroken as situations change. For example, the woman may initially want the divorce (Heartbreaker) but agrees to one more attempt with a relationship coach. While the couple is engaged in working with this professional, her partner decides it's too much work and calls it quits. She then becomes the rejected Heartbroken, and he is the initiating Heartbreaker. Not every couple does this back-and-forth dance, of course, but it does happen frequently.

When You Feel Forced to Divorce: The Heartbreaker by Default

It may be hard to tell if you are the Heartbreaker or the Heartbroken. You may have needed things in your relationship to change for a long time. Perhaps you requested that your partner change in some way, but he or she refused to acknowledge your needs. If your partner's response did not meet your expectations, you had to choose between living with a harmful situation, or ending the marriage. I've known many people who did not want to end their relationship, but they felt they had no other recourse when their partner refused to change.

The Heartbreaker by Default often experiences the emotions of both the Heartbreaker and the Heartbroken.

The Honeymoon Stage of Divorce

Many life experiences have a honeymoon period: marriage, being a new parent, a new romance, or landing the perfect job. Divorce also has a honeymoon period when all things are, relatively, rosy. You and your Ex are communicating well. There's a lot of give and take. You are *for* each other. The partner who feels guilty is very cooperative, wanting to maintain a friendship. The one who feels rejected may still be hopeful that the relationship will come back together and puts in extra effort to remain polite and unchallenging.

During this stage, it seems like getting through it will be a breeze. Like all honeymoon stages, however, it doesn't last. When papers are filed and "divorcing" begins in earnest, this honeymoon period ends. The power struggle begins.

Being "emotionally divorced for years" or legally separated is still the honeymoon stage of divorce. I've known a few people who have gotten into serious, committed, new relationships while putting off finalizing their divorces. Please understand that being in an emotionally estranged relationship and being legally divorced are two very different things. The ways you relate will change when you enter the divorce process in earnest. If you are dating someone at that time, things can turn very difficult. S/he may either ditch you along the way because you're too intense with everything you're going through, or stick it out and get hurt when your divorce completes and the new you, who may no longer be interested in the relationship, arrives on the scene and breaks things off.

Emotions as Messengers

Emotions are not stagnant. They don't just happen to you; they are messengers inviting your participation. When an emotion is present it is as though someone is knocking at your door with an important message. There are so many emotions present during divorce that it can be hard to tell which emotion is speaking—and even harder to identify the message.

If someone was screaming out to you for help: "*Help me . . . I am in pain . . . I don't know what to do . . . Do something . . . anything . . . You are the only one who can help . . .*" how would you respond? These cries are not coming from a stranger; they are coming from you. They are your emotions trying to get your attention.

In *When Things Fall Apart*, Buddhist author Pema Chödrön points out that emotions are our teachers. She says, "Generally speaking, we regard discomfort in any form as bad news . . . but for those who have a certain hunger to know what is true—feelings like disappointment, embarrassment, irritation, resentment, anger, jealousy, and fear, instead of being bad news, are actually very clear moments that teach us where it is that we're holding back. They teach us to perk up and lean in when we feel we'd rather collapse and back away. They're like messengers that show us, with terrifying clarity, exactly where we're stuck."[6]

When you approach an emotion with curiosity, rather than pushing it away or ignoring it, you can get a sense of the meaning behind it, which can lead to making better, or at least different, choices.

The table on the next page highlights emotions that are common to divorce and their potential messages. An unconscious response to an emotion can have a negative impact; those are noted on the table. When examined, each emotion also has the potential to provide an important message. The last column shows how to access the positive message.

Emotion	Used Negatively	Message	To Do
Anger	When used reactively it can cause mental and physical damage to self and others.	Reveals "shoulds" and expectations that run your life. Alerts you to an important value that has been violated. Alerts you to injustices.	Examine your beliefs. Let go of unrealistic expectations of yourself and others. Take back your power by setting limits. Ask for what you want and need but remain unattached to the response. Know that you are loved and accepted just as you are.
Fear	Immobilizes. Stops you from taking important actions or risks.	Take immediate action to stop harm; remove yourself. Take proactive steps to avoid future harm. Points to feeling unsupported by Life.	Grow past your fears. Become powerful. Take calculated risks. Trust your own abilities. Create a positive future. Pray, meditate, seek Source. Know that you are loved and accepted just as you are.
Guilt	May keep you stuck in the past. Is a legal judgment. You may believe you are worthy of the guilt.	Points out where you have violated your own values. Lets you know how much you are focusing on the past. May take on more than is yours in order to compensate.	Don't try to be perfect. Perform an autopsy of the relationship. "I did this" "S/He did that." Accept no more responsibility than that which is yours. Re-examine your values in light of current information. Take charge of your life. Know that you are loved and accepted just as you are.

Emotion	Used Negatively	Message	To Do
Hurt	Can be used to manipulate and control people who care about you. May cause you to disengage from life and other people. May cause you to be ultra-sensitive.	Reveals a need to discern who is, and is not, trustworthy. May reveal where you push people away. Reveals your perhaps unexpressed expectations of others. Points to a need for assertive action.	Become a better judge of character. Allow yourself to be supported. Set limits. Take charge of creating a positive future for yourself. Know that you are loved and accepted just as you are.
Envy	Creates discontent. You want what others have; not what you have. Causes withdrawal and judgment of others.	Reveals what you don't have but wish you did. Reveals ways you are living small.	Do what it takes to create the life *you* want. Create a positive future. Become curious instead of judgmental. Know that you are loved and accepted just as you are.
Loneliness	Causes feelings of worthlessness. May cling and smother or isolate.	Reveals the need to connect— first with self, then with others.	Learn to count on yourself. Explore inner life. Grow past fear of being alone. Create a life you love. Change negative loneliness to positive "aloneness." Know that you are loved and accepted just as you are.
Shame	Demolishes self-love and self-esteem. Has you believe something is inherently wrong with you.	Points to false messages you've believed and incorporated into your image of self.	Overwrite your "internal software" by receiving positive messages. Meet regularly with people who love and appreciate you, and who will reflect back your true essence. Know that you are loved and accepted just as you are.

Notice that the healing for each of these painful emotions is to know that you are loved and accepted just as you are. That's hard to do on your own. The remainder of this book will help. Being involved in one of our classes will help even more.

Where Are You Now?

How are you at being with your emotions?

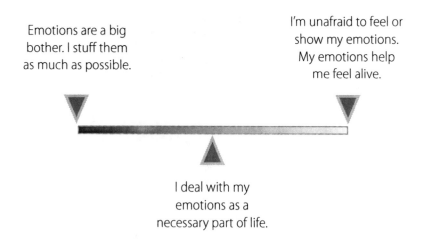

Emotions are a big bother. I stuff them as much as possible.

I'm unafraid to feel or show my emotions. My emotions help me feel alive.

I deal with my emotions as a necessary part of life.

Tears of Grief

In the midst of emotional pain,
it's difficult to imagine ever being happy.
It's difficult to see anything positive or hopeful.
The world looks bleak, dark, and dreary.
Our heart hurts with a deep, relentless ache.
All we want is to have our life, our body, our heart,
returned to fullness . . . to have our loved one back
. . . to heal the hurt . . . To heal our wounded heart.

— JOHN WELSHONS, *AWAKENING FROM GRIEF*

The loss of someone close to us can quickly turn our world into an unfamiliar place. Coping with what used to be routine becomes exhausting. The simplest task can seem daunting. All of these are symptoms of grief, the normal response to loss. It affects us not only emotionally, but also physically. Grief is emotional pain characterized by feelings of despair, helplessness, sorrow, and even rage. If you cry uncontrollably, you are not alone. If you rage at the injustice, you are not alone. If it didn't matter it wouldn't hurt. But it did matter. And it does hurt.

Most likely you were never taught how to grieve well. Most of us weren't. That leaves us on a rough sea without an oar. Most of us were taught to avoid or suppress our feelings, which is the opposite of what is useful. When our grieving skills are immature, losses hurt more than they might otherwise. Skillful grieving allows us to let go in a way that makes things better. In later chapters we will also talk about maturing our anger, boundary setting, communication, and thought-management skills. But first, let's understand the importance of grieving well and get you some relief.

The Magic in Grief

When we understand that grief also has positive aspects, we can fear it less and embrace it more. Grief is the pry bar that opens our hearts and releases our vulnerabilities. It breaks us open. It makes us softer, gentler, more compassionate people. We feel deeply connected to others who have been opened in the same ways.

There is a magic inherent in grief. If nothing else, loss and the grief connected to it cause us to appreciate the opportunities to try once more to make our life what we've wanted it to be. It's a wake-up call. There is an urgency to life, and without the wake-up call that loss brings, we might forget that.

Grieving will help you let go of that which you can't have—the relationship and other components of your life that are going away—to make room for that which you can—a new you and a better life, much of which you cannot yet envision. Think about that for a moment. Your relationship has ended, you deeply miss what once was, yet there is nothing you can do about it but let it go. It's so sobering. Grief allows us to let go in manageable pieces so we are not overwhelmed with the intensity of it all. In that, it is one of our most useful emotions.

Seeing Through the Villain and the Saint

Grieving requires letting go of both the good and the bad aspects of your former partner, the parts you loved as well as the parts you hated. Often we will remain focused on one (in divorce it is usually the bad) and ignore the other. No one is ideal and perfect; no one is absolutely evil.

It may be difficult to acknowledge that there are things you will genuinely miss about your Ex. It often feels better to hate them! In some ways, you may need to hate them in order to let go, but, at some point, you must also shed the tears associated with the loss of the tender, loving, and helpful aspects of your partner. If you're so mad that you can't see straight, you probably can't find much that is good. There must have been some good aspects, or you wouldn't have stayed in the relationship as long as you did. Acknowledging the good not only helps you let go, it allows you to acknowledge the reasons you stayed.

On the flip side, if you still feel love for your former partner, you may idealize him or her, be unable to see anything wrong with your partner's actions, or worse blame yourself.

As you heal, you will begin to acknowledge the negative and hurtful aspects of both your partner and your relationship. This will be a turning point in your return to wholeness.

One of my clients, Seth, shared this experience: *"I have been so disconnected with life and cannot remember the last time I felt connected. It is all part of the experience, and I am glad that I spent all the needed time in getting to rock bottom. It truly gave me a perspective on how much Lucy really meant to me and what a terrible loss it was to not have her in my life any-more. I realize it is fall now, or it will be soon, but I am finally beginning to metaphorically see spring—just little shades of green, for starters. And I am grateful for that."*

Grief is like a weird friend who shoots you in the foot to keep you from killing yourself. You feel the pain a little at a time. As intense as grieving is in these small doses, it is hard to fathom what the emotions of loss would feel like if we had to process them all in one sitting. It simply isn't possible. Grieving is a process, not an event. It resolves over time. There are many heartstrings to untie. It is a good thing that it is intermittent, because you need some breaks to catch your breath.

For the most part, grief tells us when we will grieve; it rarely allows us the luxury of telling it when we are ready. We may be able to stave it off for a while, but all it takes is a certain song on the radio, seeing a couple holding hands, or even a poignant message on a billboard for the sadness to kick in again. The key to successful grieving is to yield to it as much as possible when it comes. Unless you are in a place that makes it impractical, let yourself have your tears, give yourself permission to feel the feelings in all their raw-ness. Don't push them away or stuff them down.

If there are people around you who might not under-stand, try to find a way to be by yourself and let your sad-ness be there. You can go into another room or perhaps your car, or bury your head in a towel or a pillow and be with your tears. When in the presence of those who are sympathetic, sharing your feelings will help you stay pres-ent and resolve the feelings more quickly.

You may be processing other losses in addition to your relationship. It seems to work that way—one loss gets con-nected with another. This will make your grieving experi-ence more intense, so be sure you get the extra support you need. The grief of a prior loss, such as loss of a family member, may equal or surpass the grief of your current relationship loss.

Obstacles to Grieving

As silly as it sounds, grieving is an art. To grieve well we must be with it when it arises, but most of us try to avoid it at all costs. And who wouldn't? It hurts. We must keep in mind the ultimate end, which is resolved pain and a new outlook. Many things get in the way of grieving well. Here are a few:

Trying to Do All Your Grieving by Yourself

Grieving involves a process of letting go. To fully let go, it is necessary to have people around you who can hold you up—figuratively and sometimes literally. Just writing or thinking about your losses is not enough. Expressing your feelings while alone (perhaps crying in the car on your way to work) is helpful, but still not enough. To truly resolve your grief, it must be shared with at least one other person. When you share, you acknowledge its existence, its reality. By sharing, you lessen its burden. Grief will stay with you for years until you feel deeply heard by another person. Sharing honors the loss.

As you honor your grief, supportive people will come out of the woodwork. Many are happy to share their own loss experiences and support you in yours. There is a kinship, language, and community among those who share a deep experience of loss that comes no other way.

Making Up Hurtful Things about Yourself and Your Value

- Believing you are wrong, inadequate, or somehow bad because you are grieving.
- Believing you are stupid or weak, or that grieving is stupid or weak.
- Believing you should be stronger, smarter, or finished with grieving by now.
- Believing you are letting others down because you are still grieving.

Any version of these can hinder your grieving process.

Making Up Stories about What
Other People Think of You

Your grief isn't about others. It's about you. Honor yourself enough to let go of what others may think, and find peace with your own process. The bullet points above speak also to the things we believe others are saying about us. I hope you will be the one who is captain of your own team. What matters most is what *you* think of you.

Believing You've Done Your Grieving

Grieving takes as long as it takes. There is no gauge or time-line. Each situation is different. Each person is different. Merely letting time pass does not complete the process. You may have been divorced for a dozen years and be taken by surprise when feelings of loss return when watching a poignant commercial on television.

Experiencing sadness is a little like standing in a pool with the water (the sadness) just below nose level. Any splash or disruption in the water level and you're choking, perhaps drowning. Continuing to process grief allows the sadness level to drop. When it drops, figuratively speaking, to your waist, there is a lot more freedom.

It can be very useful to be in a program that provides specific exercises to help you complete the grief process. Many people in our live classes are surprised when they get in touch with feelings of grief they thought were resolved long ago. You may be doubly motivated to complete the process when you learn that any unresolved emotions will show up in, and perhaps sabotage, a future relationship.

Avoidance

If you think you should not have to go through grief, if you try to get around it, stay composed through it, don't let anyone know you're in it, or medicate it, you will slow your grieving process. If you believe that you shouldn't need to grieve or that grieving is for the weak, if you see yourself as better than, or perhaps past this necessary process, you will slow your grieving process.

Grieving is messy. It's impossible to make it look pretty. Women, you might as well give up wearing mascara, and men, you might as well ditch that tough façade and begin to embrace your tears. The more you jump in and allow yourself to feel the feelings, the faster you'll get through. You are in the process of becoming real.

Some of the things we do to stay away from the uncomfortable feelings of grief include staying busy with work or friends; excessive exercise; sex or compulsive dating; overeating; retail therapy; gambling or other addictions; distractions such as TV, movies, video games; and being an eternal student. Are there other ways you avoid your feelings?

Not all busy-ness is harmful, at least outwardly. Jana had children, a full-time job, and was working toward not one, but two doctorates while going through her divorce. It kept her away from the grief feelings, which is what she wanted, but she later realized that staying that busy had thwarted her recovery process.

Avoidance just postpones things. The feelings may go to sleep for a while, but they are there in the background and will awaken when the next loss comes along.

If substance abuse has been a challenge for you in the past, be sure to take necessary precautions during this important time. Some people attend Twelve-Step meetings every day to get themselves through. There's nothing wrong or shameful about taking care of yourself. Self-responsibility is a desirable trait and an important life skill.

Identify Your Forms of Distraction

If you have a tendency to self-medicate to avoid painful feelings, ask yourself, *What would I be feeling now if I wasn't* _____ (eating, drinking, playing video games, or whatever is your form of distraction)? If you call on your support system at such times, instead of eating or drinking or chasing another potential partner, you can resolve the emotions rather than just cover them up. Please don't be afraid to reach out to other people for support.

Stages of Grieving

Elisabeth Kübler-Ross was a medical doctor who spent a lot of time with dying people, both comforting and studying them. She wrote a book called *On Death and Dying*, which included a cycle of emotional states that is often referred to as the grief cycle. Although she identified these stages while working with death, they also apply to divorce, perhaps just not as succinctly. It's harder to complete the grieving process when there isn't a clean ending. In divorce the person you are trying to grieve is still around, often making a mess of things and reopening old wounds. Often it is helpful to declare the *relationship* dead and grieve that. When you understand the grief stages, you won't feel quite so crazy or alone in your pain. The emotions and thought processes are common to all endings.

The stages identified as the grief cycle are:

- Shock
- Denial
- Anger
- Bargaining
- Depression
- Acceptance

Let's go through this cycle as it might relate to the ending of a relationship.

Before loss hits, life is relatively stable. We don't expect that one day will be different than any other until an event takes place that knocks us out of that. We go immediately into shock.

Shock

In shock, you are like a deer in the headlights—stunned, immobile. You know something major has taken place but aren't sure of the far-reaching consequences. Maybe you went into shock when you were asked for a divorce. Maybe you went into shock when you realized that your marriage couldn't be saved. While in shock, you freeze to prevent further injury.

Denial

Denial is the inability or unwillingness to accept what has happened. Until you have the emotional resources to begin taking positive action, denial can be a place of protection. If you don't have the emotional resources to deal with the pain, keeping it safely buried under denial prevents you from being overwhelmed by things you can do nothing about. While in this stage you may have internal chatter: *"Is this really happening? Am I really getting a divorce? How can that be? No, it can't be."* If you are the heartbreaker, another version of this may be: *"Why am I doing this? Am I wrong? Am I cruel? Why can't I find another way?"* These are your attempts to come to grips with what has happened.

Considering the transition stages, shock and denial are part of the ending phase before you start healing.

Anger

After denial, you may experience the powerful emotion of anger. You may think, *"How dare s/he leave me!"* Anger is an important emotion that merits its own discussion. We will talk about the characteristics of anger in the next chapter, but for now note it as also being part of the grief cycle.

Bargaining

As you move along in your divorce process, you get a better idea of the hurts and the costs—both to your heart and your wallet. You may experience a period of back and forth as you ponder if the relationship can be saved and what it would take to save it. You may dream of the way things used to be and feel great pain when you remember that they are no longer that way. If you are in a great deal of pain, you may want desperately to reconnect with your Ex. Getting back together can seem like the quickest and best solution to the pain and sometimes that's true, but, barring special circumstances, it can make your recovery much longer. Important questions must be considered. Please see my eBook *Should We Reconcile?* for further discussion on reconciliation.

Depression

When our attempts at bargaining fail, a sober sense of reality sets in and we sink into depression. Depression is a very painful stage. It can get very dark. Some refer to it as the dark night of the soul. We wonder *Is my life worth anything? Does anyone care? How could anyone love such an abject failure?* You may feel that your life isn't worth anything, even leading you to suicidal thoughts. When in great pain, it is a natural response to want the pain to end. Suicide may seem like a viable option, but please remember that suicide is a permanent solution to a temporary problem. There are far less drastic ways to stop the pain. If you are having these thoughts I encourage you to seek help immediately. There is something about depression that numbs us to the love and care around us. It's a little like being in ice water. Perhaps it is to protect us from feeling the pain too deeply. Unfortunately, it also keeps us from feeling loved.

Eventually the numbness subsides and we can feel love again. As a matter of fact, though you probably can't fathom it right now, you will likely feel love more deeply once this cycle completes.

> **Going deeply into painful emotions makes space for us to go higher into the happy emotions. It expands our range.**

Again, your support community can keep you from going too deeply into that hole. We cannot endure a lengthy period alone in this stage. When I was in it, I had one person in my life who was the light at the end of that very dark tunnel. It made all the difference.

In the transition lens this is the In-Between Zone with its sense of being untethered. This is where we ask ourselves the big questions: *"Who am I? Does my life have any meaning? Am I worthy of love?"*

Acceptance

Eventually, and it does take a fair amount of time to untie those heartstrings, we come to accept things as they are. The pieces of life fall into place once again. In the transition lens, this is the New Beginning. We've let go of those things that no longer fit. We are presented with the opportunity to create our lives from a new perspective.

This grief model is not to be taken as a universally linear process. Stages can be skipped, experienced partially or fully, revisited, or experienced out of order. I believe that one of the reasons the grief during divorce is so intense is because we can be in different stages of grief in a variety of life areas. You may be in the depression stage as it concerns your children, the anger stage when it comes to your finances, and in the bargaining stage when it comes to your home. With all these various stages going on at one time it's no wonder you feel so out of control! The most important thing to remember is that each stage is temporary with a beginning, middle, and most importantly an end.

Working with Grief

After a major loss, your heart and soul will begin a search for things that are unfinished in an effort to complete them. Your mind will intermittently review both the positive and the negative aspects of the relationship, performing an autopsy of sorts. Divorce already has, or will, change the relationship you once had with your partner. He or she may still be around physically (which is one of the reasons divorce loss is so complicated), but you are no longer together in the same ways. An honest assessment of your ended relationship is needed so you can move on. The longer and/or more entangled your relationship was, the more involved the review process will be.

The following are a series of exercises that will help you begin to unravel your emotions, make sense of the grieving process, and gain some relief. Each exercise leads you, ultimately, to writing a letter of goodbye to your Ex that will help you find closure. I don't recommend sharing this information with your former partner. It is for your learning and healing.

Identifying Losses

Below is a partial list of losses that are common to divorce. On a separate piece of paper, or in your journal, identify the losses you are experiencing. Let those on the list inspire memories of your own. Be sure to add losses that are unique to you. Write them out in sentences or paragraphs if it helps. Be as specific as possible. Example: *"S/he got up with the kids on Saturdays so I could sleep in."* Make notes about particularly meaningful events, words, or deeds.

Financial security	Being held	My (best) friend	Future plans
The family home	My in-law family	Pets	Holidays together
My health	My peace	Date for Friday nights	Help/time with the kids
Feeling stable	Sex/touch/intimacy	Yard/gardens/shop	Mutual friends
My ability to focus	Vacations	Being happy	Memories

As an aid to seeking closure, make a list of:

- Ten things that you are genuinely going to miss about your partner
- Five behaviors, words, events of yours for which, if given the chance, you would apologize for

- Five things you wish your former partner would apologize to you for (so that you can forgive them and let them go)

- Any other type of communication to your former partner that would help with closure.

Charting Your Relationship History

This exercise will help you catalogue your relationship for review, identifying both the positive and negative aspects of your relationship so you can let go of both. As you complete your chart, do your best to remember your Ex as he or she is now, not as the person you wish she or he had been, or even once was. See the Sample Relationship History Timeline for assistance in completing yours.

To prepare your own chart you can use the blank Relationship History Timeline provided on page 89, which you can copy first (or write on the one in the book), or draw a center line the length of a sheet of paper in your journal. Follow these steps.

1. Start on the left with the date your relationship began, and end on the right with where you are now, noting the date your relationship completed. Your completion date may not necessarily be the date of your final orders. If you are still not emotionally complete, use today's date. This is your timeline.

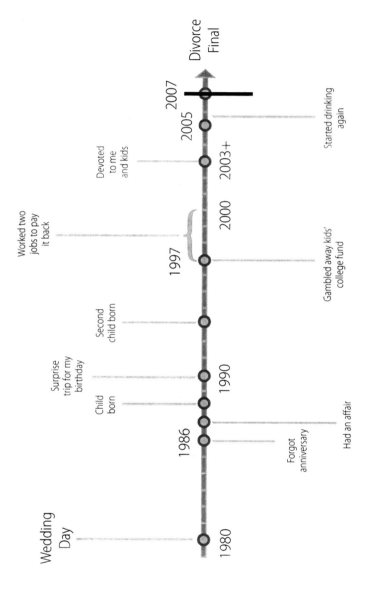

Sample Relationship History Timeline

Wedding Day

1980

1986

Forgot anniversary

Had an affair

Child born

Surprise trip for my birthday

1990

Second child born

1997

Worked two jobs to pay it back

Gambled away kids' college fund

2000

2003+

Devoted to me and kids

2005

2007

Started drinking again

Divorce Final

2. Recall both positive and negative events of your relationship. Draw perpendicular lines upward to chart positive events, and downward for negative events.

3. Make each line's length in accordance with intensity of the event, with longer lines signifying the more intense. Give the longest lines to the most positive (above) and most negative (below).

4. Mark each line with a brief note for remembrance.

5. If it is difficult to get started, begin by noting the most significant events first. It is not necessary to catalogue everything. The most pertinent events will do.

When your chart is complete, you will use it to complete the exercises that follow. Your chart will be uniquely yours and look different than the example provided.

Even though you are focusing on the things you will miss from your relationship (the positives) in this chapter on grief, events that you are angry about will also come to the surface. Include those items (the negatives) below the line for use in the anger chapter that is coming up, but don't let yourself get so sidetracked that you forget the tender and beautiful things about your relationship. You will miss those special things your partner did to show his or her love for you. You will feel angry about the betrayals and things that caused hurt instead of love. It is important to let go of both. We are purposely separating them so you can give each of

Your Relationship History Timeline

Relationship being graphed: _____ Date: _____

these powerful emotions the attention they deserve. If anger is so present that you cannot do this exercise effectively, by all means proceed to the anger chapter first and come back to this one. Just don't miss this important exercise. It is key to your healing and perhaps the most effective part of moving through turning point three.

After you have completed the above exercises, you will express them by writing two letters to your Ex, the first saying goodbye to all the things you will miss, to address the grief. And later, in the next chapter, saying goodbye to all the things you will not miss, to address the anger.

Writing Your Goodbye Appreciation Letter

Most divorcing people don't have an opportunity to express their thoughts to their Ex, and yet that can be an important part to gaining closure. Even if you can't speak directly to your spouse—or if it wouldn't provide a good outcome—nearly the same effect can be achieved by writing down your thoughts and reading them to a chosen stand-in. You will do this in the form of a letter.

Make your letter as detailed and heartfelt as possible. Include the sweet and tender things you've identified as the above-the-line items on your Relationship History Timeline, as well as your unique losses and remembrances: the happy, tender times that you shared; special things your former partner did for you; events such as holidays, children's sporting events, or plays; and things you dreamt of doing together in the future. Be as gut-level honest as you are able. This is your opportunity to say all that you would like to your former love partner.

The following letter is from a participant in one of my divorce recovery classes. Only identifiable aspects have been changed. It is used with permission. Let it inspire your own letter.

Dear Kate,

When I met you and fell in love with you, it felt like coming home. I had found the person I felt I was meant for and who I was sure I would spend the rest of my days with. Now, remarkably, I must say goodbye to that.

I think of the exceptional things about you, our relationship, and the life we have shared together . . . all things I will sorely miss.

I will miss your wit.

I will miss your laugh . . . especially when you really laugh but are trying to suppress it with your mouth closed.

I will miss swing dancing with you.

I will miss cuddling you in bed, even when it was just you backing up to me for warmth.

I will miss the touch of your hand resting on me.

I will miss our mountain excursions together. Fall will never be the same.

I will miss the tiny voice you greeted me with on the phone.

I will miss loving and adoring you. I will miss you and us.

And there are things I will always remember. I will always remember the first time I saw you, and the day in the park when I left knowing something had just changed in me.

I will always remember you showing up early in the mornings at my place to walk my dog with me.

I will always remember the weekend on the ranch and sleeping in a tiny bed with you and liking it.

I will always remember learning to enjoy antiquing with you and the trips to the small mountain towns on weekends.

I will always remember that for all its flaws, for me it was good.

I will always remember you. I will always remember us.

I know this is over. And I know that if it is the right thing for you, then it must also be the right thing for me. That doesn't make it less sad for me. Sad isn't even a strong enough word. It feels like someone has died. So, I am grieving—an appropriate reaction I am told.

This is my goodbye to all that. It is my goodbye to you, to us, to everything we ever were and everything we were ever going to be.

Thank you for what you brought to my life and for what I will take with me into my next relationship. I wish you well despite it all.

Goodbye,
George

Now it is your turn to write your letter.

After you finish writing your letter, you will read it to a trusted friend. Please don't read on until you do this important step. I know it's a book and you can do what you want. I also know you bought the book because you want to feel better. So just do it. Give yourself the gift of healing. This is the hardest, but also the most useful exercise of the entire program. Don't miss it! You have many things to say to your former partner. Now is the time.

When you finish writing, you will read your letter to your chosen stand-in. The criterion for this trusted friend is a "heart with ears,"[7] that is, someone who:

* Won't try to fix you or the situation
* Is comfortable with tears
* Won't pat you, hand you tissues, or subliminally tell you to stop crying in other ways
* Will refrain from commenting, but will demonstrate that he or she is listening
* Won't laugh, crack jokes, or tell you to get over it
* Is comfortable enough with their own losses that they won't be triggered by yours.

Tips for reading your letter:

* If the words seem to get stuck in your throat, don't swallow them. Push them up and out. Speak through the tears.
* Remember that crying is purgative. It will actually release toxins and is a form of letting go. Have plenty of tissues on hand.
* Drink a lot of water. This will soothe and calm your system and replenish lost fluids.

Note: This will stir a lot of emotions over the next several days, so take care of yourself. Have your friends' phone numbers handy and use them when you need to. Be prepared to ask for extra support at this time so you don't fall into old patterns. Set yourself up for success.

Please, do not mail your letter to your Ex. This is for you. If you don't want to keep it, you can burn it or do something ceremonious with it. Even then, be sure that you do not destroy an only copy until you are absolutely ready.

Now that you have read your goodbye letter, please stop here and take a break. You've done some hard emotional work. Go for a walk, have lunch with a friend, take a nap. Come back to the next lesson later. It will still be waiting for you when you get back. It can wait an hour, a week, or a month. It doesn't matter.

How Are You Doing?

How are you at being with your grief?

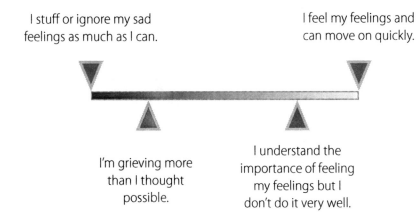

I stuff or ignore my sad feelings as much as I can.

I feel my feelings and can move on quickly.

I'm grieving more than I thought possible.

I understand the importance of feeling my feelings but I don't do it very well.

Inspirational Words on Grieving

There are some quotes that speak to me more than paragraphs ever could. Sometimes the phrase mirrors something I am feeling. Sometimes the words summarize my unformed thoughts and make them clear to me. In the quotes below, the author speaks to the role grieving plays in our journey of coming home to ourselves. I share them with the hope that something will resonate with you. If it does, you might copy it and put it in a place where you will continue to be inspired by it. You might also want to be on the lookout for other words that speak to you. They can come as quotes, song lyrics, words on a billboard, or words of a friend. It is important to surround ourselves with positive words when we can.

The real healing of grief can't take place
until we make the journey
from the mind to the heart.
And when the heart is broken,
the thought of reentering it is terrifying.
But the heart is precisely where the healing takes place.
And when it is broken, it is also wide open.

The route through the sadness is to
dive deeper into our own hearts, our own
souls, our own intuitive trust.

If I were to briefly summarize what leads
to a growthful resolution of grief,

I would say that instead of clinging to
our models of how it should have been,
or how we wish it was, we simply
turn and look at life, as it is.

If we can meet our grief with courage and awareness,
it can be the key that unlocks our hearts
and forces us into a profound new
experience of life and love.

Our work in healing grief is to redirect that
energy and to formulate a new perspective
on ourselves and on relationships
that allow for the possibility of enlightened healing,
that open the door for tragedy and suffering to
transform us into the larger
more connected, more alive beings
that, in truth, we already are.

Peace, love, and joy exist — always — in the heart, just
beneath the despair, confusion, and anger.
The perplexing reality is that the only route to joy
is through the despair, confusion, and anger.
Being fully alive requires us to be willing to feel it all.

—ALL QUOTES BY JOHN WELSHONS[8]

10

The Fire of Anger

Anyone can become angry — that is easy,
but to be angry with the right person at the right time,
and for the right purpose and in the right way —
that is not within everyone's power
and that is not easy.

— ARISTOTLE

O f all our emotions, anger is the most confusing. We all have anger, few of us want it, and even fewer of us know what to do with it. Often, it just makes things worse. Some important questions arise: What is the purpose of anger? How can we make good use of it? And most importantly, how can we manage the extreme anger that is common to divorce?

Being in touch with our anger is ultimately a good thing, although initially it may not seem that way. People are often afraid that their anger will take over or that they will explode and hurt someone. That is rare. It is because we are unfamiliar with our anger and we have pushed it away that it seems so big. We can't perceive the edges of it, so we imagine it to be without end.

You may have so much anger that it feels completely unmanageable and you are looking for relief. There is something about the level of betrayal, broken promises, and irresponsible actions of the partners we thought we knew that elicits a deeper, seething response than what we experience in daily living. The person who promised to love you is now actively hurting, hindering, or betraying you. *"How dare they?"* It's all so unfair. These behaviors elicit sometimes crippling, sometimes violent, feelings. It's the kind of anger that makes you want to hurt somebody, destroy things, slash tires. This is the extreme anger of divorce, and this kind of anger takes special management. We have some solutions for that, but first let's learn a little more about what anger is.

The Purpose of Anger

Anger is your alarm system. When it is working well, anger will alert you if one of your boundaries is crossed or an important value has been violated. Perhaps you recall one of those times right now.

One of the most common sources of anger for divorcing people is the feeling that things are not fair. For example, if your soon-to-be Ex is spending money on fancy vacations while you don't have two nickels to rub together, you may see red. Sometimes anger just isn't a strong enough word for the emotion you feel when your Ex lies about you to your children, or hides assets, or loves someone else. There's nothing like a significant betrayal to turn indifference to hate.

The energy of anger can provide the impetus you need to set those important limits, push back, or leave a dangerous situation. It can also provide the energy you need to take care of yourself and to attend to the wounds that have accrued over the time when you didn't set those important limits. Unfortunately, your alarm system may not work as well as it should, leaving you vulnerable to hurtful situations.

The energy of anger is meant to empower us to solve problems and heal our injuries. In divorce there are few relational problems left to solve. Our former partner is not interested in working things through, or, often, even stopping the behaviors that have hurt us so much. They may not even be aware of the ways they have hurt us. John Rifkin in his book *The Healing Power of Anger* states that anger is a source of personal power and that all problems, as well as all anger, begin with an injury. Anger is the natural healing energy that the body generates in order to attend to the injury.

The Anger Spectrum

What is your anger style? Are you fiery and hot? Loud and destructive? Passive and cold? Sneaky and manipulative? Or out of touch with your anger entirely?

People generally have one of two styles when on the receiving end of harmful behavior. One is to react with deep sadness and take the emotions *inward*, which is one source of depression. This causes harm to the vessel of your body.

The second style is to react with powerful anger and lash *outward* and onto others. It can be frightening or threatening to witness this kind of anger.

Perhaps it wasn't safe for you to express anger in your family so you learned to ignore it or stuff it away. You may have expressed it through innocent-looking but hostile ways known as passive-aggressive behavior. A passive person is afraid of his or her anger and does not know how to speak up and use it proactively. Instead anger is expressed in indirect ways like snide comments, burning the toast, or "forgetting" to pick up the clothes from the dry cleaners. Because passive-aggressive behaviors are indirect, it is sometimes difficult to understand their angry roots.

Perhaps your example at home was constant fighting or even abuse. You didn't learn effective ways to settle disputes or approach upsetting situations so your default response is anger. Many men respond in anger when other emotions would be more appropriate. It's unfortunate that the "man code" has been such that anger has been the most acceptable emotion available to men. Thankfully men are allowing themselves more emotional range.

Where Are You on the Spectrum of Anger?

Anger can be mapped on a spectrum like you see on page 101.

- Place an X where you are.
- Notice that the ideal range is in the center.

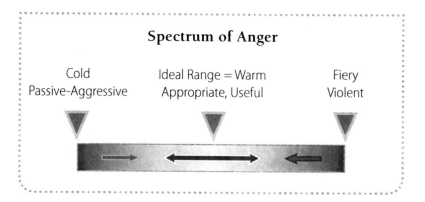

As anger matures, the ends of the spectrum will move closer to the center range of appropriate, useful anger. This is difficult to do for those at both extremes for different reasons.

The person with cold, passive anger is frightened by coming closer to the heat of appropriate anger. Feeling the heat, s/he fears being mean or hurting people, the heat of a fiery temper, or even her own assertiveness. It is very common for those with passive anger to try hard to keep others happy so they don't have to deal with the anger. Without conscious observation and a willingness to move closer to the center, this fear can keep a person in a passive position for a lifetime.

On the other side of the spectrum, the person with hot, fiery anger is frightened by the coolness of appropriate anger. To let go of the fiery anger is interpreted as giving up power and control. S/he may feel weak and vulnerable as s/he moves toward the ideal range, and, without conscious observation, react to this feeling of impotence with more rage.

You can begin to mature your anger by choosing mature anger responses as listed below. Also work at developing a tolerance for the uncomfortable feelings you experience when you move out of your position and closer to center. Be willing to live with that discomfort while you shift to a more workable style.

Learning Anger

Most of us have come to believe that anger is dangerous in some way. This is usually learned in childhood under one of two conditions:

- Anger has made love go away. You (or someone you cared about) received the silent treatment, was shamed, or perhaps was shunned for expressing anger.
- You (or someone you cared about) experienced some form of angry attack physically, verbally, or both.

If you had one parent who shamed or shunned you for expressing anger while the other parent attacked in some way, the conflicting messages make it even more difficult to untangle. Anger is modeled for us in many ways. Let's explore the roots of your beliefs about anger.

What Did You Learn About Anger?

What did you learn about anger in the family you grew up in? Here are some possibilities:

- It's okay for adults to show anger but not kids.

- It's okay for boys to show anger but not girls.

- People won't like me if I'm angry.

- Anger always hurts people.

What did you learn from society (schools, TV, church, athletics) about dealing with anger? Here are some possibilities:

- Nice people don't get angry.

- Being angry is a sign of weakness.

- If I get angry it causes more anger to come back at me.

- People justify their own anger but condemn me when I'm angry.

- If I get angry, I get benched/dismissed/punished or attacked.

Are any of those true for you? Take a moment to write down and describe your own lessons. How was anger modeled for you? What do you believe about anger today because of your childhood messages? How is this affecting your divorce?

Mature and Immature Anger

Most of us were not taught as children how to use anger in positive ways. Much of what we saw was immature, amounting to little more than a tantrum. Maturing in anger[9] and using it effectively is an important skill that allows us to take a focused and assertive stance toward relationship problems rather than allow the seething ball of emotion to eat us up inside.

Most of us come to divorce with immature anger because we've had so little instruction on its appropriate use throughout our lives. We may be forty-seven years of age, but we may be much younger when it comes to anger. That makes the anger we experience while divorcing all the more difficult. Going through the divorce process matures us in many ways. As you mature in anger, you will be less fearful, more trusting, and will more easily recognize the choices before you. The goal of healthy anger is to protect you and those you care about. It is not about attack or revenge.

The following chart shows characteristics of immature anger contrasted with mature anger, as taught by Dr. Henry Cloud and Dr. John Townsend, clinical psychologists and authors of the best-selling book *Boundaries*. It will help you identify where you are. After reviewing it, you will see that those who are mature in anger:

- Relate to others as equals
- Speak directly and honestly to self and others
- Know the end goal is not about fighting, arguing, making one's point, or being right

■ Know how to manage the energy of anger
and use it as a tool for good

■ Know that the goal of life is love, and use
anger proactively to protect it.

Maturing happens over time. It takes inner strength to
let go of the desire to retaliate or control others, to learn
to take responsibility and speak assertively, and to develop
enough emotional strength to hold the other in love, or at
least in respect, while we are angry.

Young Anger	Mature Anger
Blames others, rather than recognizing own power in a situation. Feels like a victim.	Takes responsibility.
Difficulty telling the truth; lies and stutters.	Speaks directly and honestly.
Object of anger is vague. Anger just there in the background, spilling into everything.	Is specific. Knows what s/he is angry about.
Reactive; comes up each time buttons are pushed. Feels mad instead of sad. May blow up when feeling helpless. Anger becomes a default response to many emotional situations.	Active or proactive, goes after solutions.
Still attempting to control the other.	Has good self-control; has given up the fantasy of controlling the other.
Can't feel close and mad at the same time. Believes "I am all bad, or you are all bad."	Can experience anger and closeness at the same time. Understands that people are a combination of both good and bad traits.
Goal is to get revenge. "I want to hurt or maybe even annihilate you."	Goal is a positive solution. "I am going to protect myself, but I am also advocating for a good outcome."

Mature anger alerts us to the need to take responsibility for ourselves and the situation, to speak honestly about what we need or want, to set limits, and to protect ourselves while advocating for the best outcome. This is an important part of the second turning point.

Healthy Blame

Both you and your Ex contributed to the demise of your relationship, and learning your part will empower you. If you can incorporate what you learn about your part early enough, it may serve you during your divorce process. Owning up to even some of your stuff and, when possible, acknowledging it to your spouse, can diffuse some of the negative energy around a trying mediation or other divorce negotiation. It can also make it easier for your Ex to own up to his or her part.

When I speak of healthy blame I am referring to an internal diagnostic process to help you identify what went wrong in your ended relationship—an autopsy of sorts. *"Okay, I see that I did _____. I don't like that I did it and I want to change. But darn it s/he did _____."* Use this time to examine your destructive behaviors and take ownership for them. Write about them in your journal or talk to supportive friends about what you learn. Let your feelings of blame be diagnostic and temporary, not a place you reside.

Assessing Healthy Blame

1. Name five things you blame your partner for.

2. Name five problems that you contributed to.

3. Looking at things now, how much blame do you attribute to your partner, yourself, and the dynamics between the two of you for the collapse of your relationship? For example, I blame my partner for 45%, myself for 20%, and both of us together for 35%. (Please don't get stuck on exact numbers. These don't have to add up to 100%.) You might want to revisit this question from time to time to see how your answer shifts.

Where Are You?

How are you assigning blame?

| I blame myself for everything. | I have identified several things for which we are each to blame. | I blame my partner for everything. |

A Word about Revenge

When the love we need to survive is abruptly taken from us, we may react in ways that surprise even us. It is as if something has taken over and all we can think about is the way we've been wronged. *"This shouldn't be!"* We want our partner to know how badly s/he is hurting us. We want them to hurt as deeply as we are hurting, and we may have vengeful thoughts, or want to take vengeful actions to make sure that happens.

Maybe you are reviewing your relationship with a scorecard. *"Look at all the things I did for him/her. How dare s/he leave without giving back."* It hurts to be left hanging, especially when we were counting on a return on our past investment. Keeping a scorecard might feel better for a little while, but ultimately it does little more than provide fuel for keeping the anger alive. You need other alternatives.

Ultimately you will want to provide the love, affection, admiration, respect, and other things you expected from your partner, for yourself. This takes some skills you don't yet have, so until you are able to provide for yourself you will need to get those things from other people. It may seem like your partner is the only person who can make you feel better, but in actuality the love, affection, and respect you need can come from other sources. It is important to develop friendships where those things are present. I hope you won't do without those things while protesting how things are.

Working with Anger

Anger's unique gift is that it provides us with breadcrumbs to follow it back to its source where we can then resolve it with some focused effort. If anger is overpowering for you, I suggest enlisting a specialist to help you identify the source of your anger, and the feelings it is trying to protect you from. An injured animal will lash out when it is wounded. We do that, too. Anger is a cover emotion. That is, it covers other things that we are unaware of or unwilling to acknowledge such as a sense of inadequacy, fear of abandonment, disappointed expectations, sadness, and other vulnerabilities. All are rooted in some form of not having our needs met.

We may lash out in anger, or react to someone else's anger from a lifetime of painful experiences collected inside. The "pain body" (accumulation of memory of past slights) is triggered. If you couldn't, or didn't, push away painful experiences in the past, a part of you may react forcefully, as it should have back then. This pain body has a life of its own with a strong desire to survive just like any other being. It has the ability to rise up and live through you, reacting in most inappropriate ways toward you and toward others. It can be loud and aggressive, or small and whiney. It can be emotionally violent, physically violent, or both. Acknowledging its presence may calm it. You might let your adult parts ask it what it needs. Often it just wants to be heard and the simple act of asking the question calms it.

Several exercises follow that will help you learn from, release, and proactively use the energy of anger for useful purposes.

There are two basic approaches to releasing anger. One involves active, physical discharge; the other is to release the anger by focusing on its opposite, which is inner peace and a meditative practice of non-attachment.

Releasing Anger Physically

Below are a few examples of active physical release. You may have more creative ideas of your own.

Using a punching bag	Pounding bread dough
A pounding run on a treadmill	Kickboxing
Weight lifting	Demolition work
Shredding things	Throwing paint on a canvas
Screaming into a pillow	Any physical activity until you're too tired

If you are experiencing powerful anger you may need more intense forms of release. You might try some of the exercises below. Remember that anything that releases the charge without hurting anyone or anything is free game. The exercise below are more pointed, but still harmless. Make sure your children don't see you participating in anything that denigrates their other parent.

- Driving your car with your Ex's picture on the tire.
- Putting your Ex's picture on the bottom of your shoe and running or wearing it for the day.
- Visualizing your Ex's face on a punching bag, the pillow you beat, or dough you pound.
- Boxing up anything that reminds you of your Ex for return or pickup.

You can use anything that releases the energy and doesn't cause harm to you or someone else. As an example, Gloria went home after the anger session in one of our live classes and with great fanfare and physical gusto shredded the comforter from what had been their marriage bed. She then tied it in knots for the dogs to play with. This is a great example of a physical release that hurts no one.

Make sure your children are absent during what could be a powerful and scary activity for them. No child wants to see their parent exorcising their anger. This is too complex a situation for them to understand.

Releasing Anger through Non-Attachment

Here are examples of more passive activities used to dissolve or replace anger:

- Use meditative or spiritual practice to replace the anger with peaceful thoughts.

- Create distance from your anger by observing it. (See "Be The Watcher" on page 112.)

- Use anger as a signal to become present.

- Speak positive and affirming words to yourself, instead of focusing on anger.

- Actively work at forgiveness.

- Allow yourself to be supported by friends who can put the latest stressful event into perspective.

None of these techniques will work every time. Do what works in the moment. Know that you have many tools in your toolbox for dealing with this important emotion. Take a minute to identify several approaches you can use to discharge or minimize anger in the future.

Be The Watcher

Being able to observe our actions, reactions, and behavior is an important skill. It works especially well when it comes to managing anger. When we *observe* that we are angry, we aren't taken over by it. *"Wow. I am feeling intensely angry right now"* is one step removed from *being* the anger. You've created a level of separation.

The Watcher is another aspect of your True Self, the part of you that observes the happenings of your life from a non-reactive place. It takes some awareness to access this part of ourselves, but it is powerful when we do.

A simple exercise to help you become aware of The Watcher is to observe your breathing. As you breathe in and out, silently and rhythmically, notice that there are two involved: the one breathing, and the one observing the one breathing. If you are the one breathing, who is doing the watching? It is your higher consciousness. Remember that this core self is always peaceful, never fearful, and is the fountain of all wisdom. When we are able to view life from a place of peace, love, and wisdom, anger is no longer necessary. We realize that anger is little more than a reaction to our life circumstances. It is worth the effort to develop this skill.

Saying Goodbye to the Things You Won't Miss

In the grief chapter you wrote a letter acknowledging the things you will miss from your relationship, the above-the-line items on the Relationship History Timeline. In this exercise you will say goodbye to the things you will not miss about your partner and the relationship. These are the items below the line on your Timeline, the hurtful and abusive things your partner did, the lies and betrayals, the ways he or she was not there for you during your relationship and is not there for you now. These are the things that make you damn angry.

In our in-person divorce recovery classes I give participants a three-foot sheet of butcher paper and a variety of crayons—red is a favorite—to write their anger letter. This engages the child-mind and also provides a whole-body experience, instead of just an intellectual one. Write your anger letter in whatever way suits you. I don't recommend using the computer for this exercise, as that takes too much of the emotion out of it.

This is a multi-step process:

1. Review the below-the-line items on your Relationship History Timeline.

2. Read the following sample letter.

3. Write your Anger Letter.

4. Read your letter to a trusted friend, therapist, or coach.

This sample Anger Letter was written by a former class participant. Identifiers have been changed. It is used by permission to give you an idea of the different things you might write about. This is one person's experience; yours will be different. I encourage you to write from your gut. Tap into the depths of your disappointment and hurt. Don't hold back! Feel free to use profanity if it helps. This is your letter!

Dorothy,

Why were you always so angry with me? Apparently, there was only enough room for one hurt in our relationship, and you claimed it. I never had a chance.

Well, I'm angry at you for blaming me for everything you felt wrong in your life. I tried so hard to listen and make our marriage work. My marriage, my family meant everything to me. Yet you were addicted to the self-absorbed comfort you felt from being "the victim."

I'm angry at you for the steady stream of suicide threats. I'm angry for all of the self-mutilation, the cutting, the threatening behavior with knives. I'm angry about the times I had to call the police. I'm sure the neighbors thought it was domestic violence.

I'm angry that you habitually threatened divorce throughout our marriage, the way a bully repeats a behavior that satisfies. You knew how much that hurt me. I loved you so much but seemed unable or incapable of making you understand that.

I'm angry that you transferred our life savings into secret accounts in your name and hid the paperwork. I'm angry that you got furious at me when I discovered your deception. You never understood the violation of trust. I'm angry at how you bullied me, then always explained it in a way that you were the victim. Always the victim.

I'm angry at how you used our children. You told them that I hit you, and you knew you were lying. How could you tell them that? Despite the many times you struck me, I could never strike you, and you understood that. Yet honesty was never a priority with you. I guess victims get special dispensation to create their own reality. But how could you use your children like that? I guess you would do anything to hurt me.

I'm angry that you insisted I fix myself with professional help or—that's right, you were going to divorce me. You were fine. I was the one who needed help. I begged you to go to marriage counseling, but you refused. You said "Everyone knows you don't go to counseling with an abuser." Always the victim. I'm angry at how willing your therapist was to say things to bring you back for the next $100 session. I'm angry at how willing you were to throw me under the bus to satisfy your own egocentric need to be the victim.

I'm so angry at you for the dishonesty and lies, before, during, and after the divorce. I'm angry at the hypocrisy. You are so different to everyone else. You rage at those you claim to love, and you perform brilliantly for those you want to like you.

Jim

Take out your journal or other paper and begin your Anger Letter now. When you are finished, read your Anger Letter to a trusted friend. In this case, the listener should be someone who:

- Won't try to fix you or the situation.

- Won't try to calm you or preach to you, but will listen, encourage, and perhaps even champion you, especially if expressing anger is hard for you.

- Is comfortable enough with their own anger that they won't be triggered or react when experiencing yours.

Next, decide what to do with your letter. Sending it to your Ex is not a good idea. That just escalates things. As tempting as it is, I hope you will refrain. If you want to destroy it, please do so creatively and safely. Make sure you don't destroy an only copy until you're ready. If you've spoken negatively in your letter about your child's other parent, do whatever you need to do to make sure your child *never* sees it! I cannot emphasize the importance of this enough.

Be prepared to experience more feelings of anger over the next week or so. This is a normal response. You've stirred up a lot of feelings. As is the case with all emotional resolution, contact your support community to share and receive support. And, as always, be gentle with yourself.

Hopefully, your letter brought your anger out into the open and let you see it at face value. Perhaps this is the first time you've experienced your anger to such a degree. Reading your letter to your trusted friend may have helped dissipate some of the intensity, but anger is such a strong emotion, and is recreated in so many ways when ending a relationship that it will take ongoing focused effort to release it.

Before Anger Strikes

Sometimes anger blindsides us. We don't see it coming. At other times we can feel the anger rising and can change something, such as leave the restaurant, hang up the phone, or change the subject before it takes us over. Here are a few other ideas.

Tips for Being Proactive with Anger

- Be alert to the presence of anger. Avoid situations where your anger alarm is likely to be triggered.

- Learn about yourself by looking at what makes you angry. When you know the values that are being stepped on, you can proactively protect them rather than reactively defend them.

- Develop coping strategies for handling your anger, including assertive communication, relaxation, physical exercise, meditation, removing yourself from an adverse situation, being in nature, expressing to a friend.

- Be appropriately assertive in asking for

what you want and need. Assertive behavior includes what you say and how you say it. Ask for what you want and set your limits in a way that is neither hostile nor aggressive, including limits you set with your voice and body language. Be clear and direct in a way that respects both you and the other person.

■ Learn the differences between mature and immature anger. Choose mature responses as much as possible.

■ Own the anger as yours. Others can't make you angry. If you didn't have those feelings inside you, the person could not elicit or hook into them.

■ Talk things out so you don't have to act them out. Learn to communicate without blaming by using "I" statements such as *"I want," "I feel," "I need,"* rather than *"you never," "you always," or "you don't."*

■ Stay current. Don't allow your resentments to build on each other. It will be easier on you and allow for a better outcome if you handle one issue at a time.

■ Spend time with people who like you and encourage the best in you. People who don't feel good about themselves often feel they don't have the right to be angry or react strongly out of defensiveness.

Tips for Living an Anger-Free Life

Additionally, there are things you can do to promote a more anger-free life. Here are a few:

- Adopt positive attitudes toward life. Try viewing the world as a nurturing womb or benevolent friend who wants only the best for you.
- Listen to and practice trusting others.
- Practice kindness.
- Maintain a sense of humor about yourself and others.
- Look for the best in others and the best in life; what you focus on tends to grow.
- Practice gratitude.
- Use adverse situations as reminders to become present.
- Forgive. Let go of your need to blame.
- Be proactive in seeking solutions.
- Focus on creating a happy life.
- Any of the meditative practices mentioned earlier.

It may be useful to plan ahead which strategies to use when working through angry situations.

Where Are You Now?

How are you doing with anger?

My anger is out of
control. It seems
to run me more
than I run it.

I know how to use
anger to confront
situations and
solve problems.

I stuff my anger
away. It just causes
problems.

I do pretty well expressing
my anger but I'm still
reactive and explosive, or
I stuff it more than I want.

The Burden of Guilt

No audience is needed for feelings of guilt,
no one else need know,
for the guilty person is his own judge.

—PAUL EKMAN, *TELLING LIES*

Guilt is a weighty emotion. It feels like dragging a refrigerator around with you. It gets in the way, slows you down, hinders you from thinking about other things, and wears you out. Although both you and your partner probably feel some guilt for the way things turned out or for the impact of your divorce on others, the person ending the relationship usually feels it most.

Like all emotions, guilt has a message. If you feel a strong sense of responsibility toward caring for your partner, perhaps believing they cannot care for themselves in some way such as financially or emotionally, you will feel a tremendous amount of guilt for leaving them in what you believe to be a helpless state.

Guilt also alerts you that you have violated one or more of your strongest values. Perhaps you were committed to keeping your marriage together, and when you couldn't, were overcome by guilt. If you ended your relationship, you likely didn't do it on a whim. You were probably hurting or discontent for quite some time. Perhaps you had to choose between keeping your relationship intact and compromising yourself. Or maybe you just heard the beat of a different drum and knew it was time to change directions. It would be nice to meet *our* needs along with the needs of others, but sometimes that just isn't possible. Life takes twists and turns that we don't anticipate. It requires things of us that we don't have the knowledge or the skills to deal with. Hard decisions must be made.

Guilt keeps us in a constant state of inquiry. You may wonder if you are doing the right thing, or how you can purposely hurt those you proclaim to love. You may be worried about what your friends, parents, or spiritual community will think. All of this mind activity is an attempt to reconcile your beliefs and your actions. Some of it is a normal part of the process, but it can get out of control and result in unnecessary pain. We often give it too much power.

Guilt is especially painful for those with a strong inner critic who takes very seriously its job of upholding rules. You may feel a pang of guilt any time you try to assert yourself or even *think* about doing something that your internal voice would say is wrong. If you feel that you're being mean when you stand up for yourself, get a second opinion from a friend. Most times you will find that your actions are completely appropriate.

Healthy Guilt

A little guilt is a good thing. It is part of a healthy conscience. Heeding that little voice keeps us within acceptable personal and societal boundaries. When these boundaries are crossed, guilt acts as an emotional shock collar to get us back in line. We train our conscience throughout our lives by the rules we internalize. The rules can be reasonable and good, which keeps us safe, or they can be extreme and limiting. If they are too limiting, we won't take the risks necessary to get out of a hopeless situation or do what we need to do to create a great life. At the extreme, an overactive conscience can punish us harshly, often for the wrong things. We will talk more about the harsh inner critic in a later chapter. After your conscience has been programmed, it will operate according to the parameters you've given it. Part of growing up is sorting through the rules, keeping those that make sense and amending or eliminating those that don't.

Common Sources of Guilt While Divorcing

It is common to experience a certain amount of guilt while divorcing. We've broken promises to ourselves and to others, and our inner guidance is firing. Below are some common sources of guilt.

Feeling Responsible for the Pain of your Former Partner

If you are an over-responsible type, you may be carrying

the burden of guilt for both you and your former partner. It is important to discern what is yours and what isn't. You have enough challenges of your own without trying to take on your Ex's burdens, too. If you can't decide what you are truly responsible for, ask your friends for their more objective viewpoint. Own and take care of what you can, and give your Ex the opportunity to deal with his or her own feelings. Sometimes life is painful and there's nothing that can be done about that.

Taking on the Guilt Others Place on You

Perhaps your Ex won't take responsibility for his or her part in the ended relationship. Sometimes people can't see their part for a long time, even if they want to. For a victim to remain a victim, there has to be a villain, and you may be the likely candidate for your former mate. You needn't accept this role out of a sense of guilt. Your Ex may be projecting his or her own guilt onto you because s/he can't bear it. You certainly don't need to take on any guilt that isn't yours. You have enough of your own. Look honestly at your part and let the rest go.

Believing You Should Have Done Better

It is important to remember that you did your best, given who you were and what you knew at the time. Maya Angelou says, "If you should have done better, you would have done better." You didn't know then what you know now. If you had it to do over again you would do the same because it was the best choice for you at the time.

Perfectionism

Too often we set unrealistically high standards for ourselves, and when we don't live up to them we feel guilty. Gina searched for months for the perfect answer to her difficult situation. Her husband wanted her to come home, but he refused to acknowledge that there were problems in the marriage. She didn't know how to save her marriage and her family without compromising what she needed in the relationship. That she couldn't find the answer was a continual source of guilt. After a long and difficult period, she reluctantly accepted that there was no magic solution and that she had to choose her own well-being. Sometimes, there is no right answer. None of us knows the perfect thing to do all the time. Once we accept that, life becomes easier. We make the best choice we can and make adjustments as needed.

Solution for Guilt: Examine Your Values

Since guilt alerts us to values we've violated, it serves us to identify those values so we can re-examine them. Sometimes we find that the violation is of a "law" from childhood that no longer applies. For example: *"I have to be good."* What does that mean? Yes, there was some sort of yardstick by which you were measured as a child, but is it applicable and a true measure, now?

Look at Your Values

If you are suffering from guilt, examine the values you believe you have violated. Write them down. List as many as you can. Examples could be: *I will never get divorced. I will not hurt others. I will not disappoint my mother or father.* It is often the unidentified beliefs that plague us the most, so keep writing until you've uncovered even the silliest example. Looking at your list, identify the rules that really make sense given who you are today. Then identify the rules that have been running like a default program in the background that are no longer useful.

Of the values you believe you've violated, which are causing you the most pain? Test them with these questions:

- Is this value I'm hanging onto one I've chosen as an adult or one that's left over from childhood?
- Does this rule make sense today or should I just delete it?
- Is this my value or someone else's? A parent, school bully, church doctrine, etc.?
- Is it realistic to expect this of myself, even on my best days?
- Have I done my best to live up to this value?
- What do I need in order to let myself off the hook?

Solution for Guilt: Be Aware of Your Judgments

Guilty is a legal judgment. The gavel is dropped and the pronouncement is made. Yet, even without a hearing, we judge ourselves and others, often without evidence. Former partners often judge one another, each thinking the other should be doing better. We pronounce our Ex guilty, a jerk, thief, bum, crazy, an idiot, and a whole host of other labels. We may not notice it initially, but we will judge ourselves with the same labels. Labels are a seemingly innocent, yet deadly, way to judge.

The truth is, your Ex has many positive characteristics that may be difficult for you to acknowledge. Hopefully you identified some of those while working in the grief chapter. Notice your tendency to see your Ex in only one way. Notice your tendency to see yourself in limiting ways. *"I'm bad, wrong, a jerk, broken, a bad mother/father . . ."* whatever it is. A negative label can be hard to live down. Know that you are the one who is doing the labeling and you can choose to stop, or choose a more positive label, at any time. There's something magic about choosing to think better about someone; almost miraculously we begin to think better about ourselves, too.

If you feel guilty you may say things to yourself like, *"How can I be happy if I'm making others so unhappy?"* I've seen people tolerate a variety of punishing behaviors in an attempt to appease their guilt. You may not be aware that you're doing it because it can seem so right. Consider the times you say, "I don't deserve . . ." *I don't deserve to be happy. I don't deserve half of our marital assets. I don't deserve the love of my children. I don't deserve great friends. I don't deserve a good relationship.* On and on it goes. Do you feel you don't deserve these things because you are *guilty* of causing pain?

We don't earn these things by being "good," so does it make sense that we should lose them by being "bad"? As adults, we understand that Santa's good and bad lists are fiction. Imperfection is a fact of life. If you made a mistake, own it, learn from it, rectify what you can, and move on. Remove that splinter of guilt that causes needless pain. Continuing to punish yourself won't do you any good, and it certainly won't do your children any good. Maybe the best thing you can give your children is the gift of your self-forgiveness.

Notice Self-Judgments

Watch your mind. Notice your tendency to judge yourself and your former partner. Notice when, where, and how you do it. Notice how you feel about yourself and your Ex when you do it. After a couple of weeks of observing in this way, make an effort to stop. Do an experiment to see if the guilt feelings lessen when the judging stops.

Solution for Guilt: Live in the Present

Reliving past events provides many opportunities to keep the guilt alive and flog yourself for the choices you made. You remember when things were good, when the family enjoyed holidays or vacations together, when you felt loved and supported, and you realize those things will never happen in the same way again. That hurts. A friend reminded me that our memories live in us. You can have them with you, right now, wherever you go.

Some memories are too special to allow them to fade, but living in the past is a high price to pay. I recently took an extended road trip. At several points on my journey I had cars following too closely so I kept a careful eye on them in my rearview mirror. After a while I realized that I'd traveled a good portion of my journey looking behind me. Focusing on the driver behind me was the entirety of my experience. I missed all the beautiful sites I was driving through. Many of us do in our daily lives. We focus on the pain and confusion of the moment and miss the beauty all around us.

Being Present

Right now, in this moment, close your eyes. Breathe quietly until you feel a stillness in and around you. It may take several minutes, especially if your mind isn't used to this type of stillness. Don't give up. Once you've found the stillness, ask "Is there anything to feel guilty about in this moment?" If you feel that there is, examine your thoughts again. Are they darting back to the past or into the future? If you truly access this present moment, guilt will be gone. There is nothing for you to feel guilty about right here, right now.

Solution for Guilt: Let Go of How It Ought to Be

Most of us have a standard in our head about how things should go, how we should be, and of what we should be capable. Yet this is just an idea in our head; there is no standardized scale by which people are measured. Comparison itself is risky; perhaps the most constructive use for our concern is watching for our own personal best.

Letting go of guilt is accomplished by unconditionally accepting your current situation and abilities, whatever they may be. Letting go of guilt around what you do or do not know is an important first step. As you continue to grow, you will have access to better solutions.

Put Down the Whip

List ten things you believe you *should* or *should not* be doing. Now, look at your list through the lens of what you are going through, the resources you have, the betrayals you feel, the fears you are facing, the worries that you carry, and decide if, given all those circumstances, you really should be doing better. No, you say? You're doing the very best you can, you say? Then what is there to feel guilty about? Give yourself a break.

Where Are You Now?

What level of guilt are you feeling?

| Guilt is eating me up. Sometimes I think that's all I feel. | Sometimes I remember that I don't have to feel guilty. | I have worked through my guilt and let it go. |

12

Paralyzing Fear

I will face my fear. I will permit it to pass over me
and through me. And when it has gone past,
I will turn the inner eye to see its path.
Where the fear has gone there will be nothing.
Only I will remain.

—FRANK HERBERT, *DUNE*

The most pervasive emotion in the divorce process, the one that will drive your worst decisions and cause your worst nightmares, is fear. The fear in divorce goes beyond common human experience; in that, it is traumatic. An adventurer who finds herself in a life-threatening situation may experience a similar level of fear, but by and large, day-to-day life just doesn't present us with the kind of fear we face in divorce. You're afraid, the kids are afraid, your soon-to-be-Ex is afraid and doing the craziest stuff. The In-Between Zone is rife with fear. This fear stops you cold. You feel numb, paralyzed, and isolated. You can't think clearly. You don't know which direction is the right one, so you don't choose any at all. This is the fear that throws you into survival mode.

When we're afraid, we are convinced that there isn't enough. There isn't enough love. There isn't enough money. There aren't enough hours in the day to be with the kids, make some money, get the laundry done. When we are convinced there isn't enough and that we aren't enough, we are afraid. Fear undermines confidence and trust. Fear would have you believe that you will perish before anything good comes your way. You look out and see nothing but rough seas—or an abyss.

In addition to the general fears surrounding your divorce, you may be aware of deeply rooted fears that have been with you, perhaps even since childhood. Having a partner by your side may have kept those fears at a manageable level, but now that your partner is gone those raw fears may rise up again. You may be asking yourself:

- Where did this intense fear come from?
- Why do I feel so utterly alone?
- What is this something inside me that feels orphaned?

If this is true for you, I hope you will let your divorce—or more accurately your recovery from divorce—be an opportunity to heal any past wounding, once and for all.

There are a number of things you can do to manage fear. I will talk about several: identifying fears, choosing love, neutralizing fear, controlling your thoughts, staying present, and taking charge of what you can. Each works in a different way. One may be more effective for you than another. You may be tempted to just read through the exercises rather than apply them, but you will gain more benefit by participating. I hope you will choose one or two to work through.

Solution for Fear: Identifying Your Fears

Do you fear your future? This is probably the most common fear for a person whose most significant relationship has ended. You look to the landscape ahead and see only a bank of fog—or worse, a cliff. Where do you turn? Which is the right course?

Identifying Your Fears

Below is a list of common fears that people going through a divorce face. As you read, make note of yours, and add other fears you have that are not on the list. Writing them down gets them out of your head and creates some much-needed distance. They won't seem as big and impossible when written down.

- **Fear of being able to make it outside of marriage**. If you've always been in a relationship you may wonder how you will ever make it as a single person.

- **Fear of being alone, both now and in old age**. For most divorcing people the thought of being alone as they age is just short of terrifying. And yet the thought of one day dating again—and the possibility of being hurt again—is also overwhelming.

- ■ **Fear of being found out.** When married, our relationship struggles are kept behind closed doors, but in divorce it feels as if our lives are on display for all to see. Until we are able to let it go, there is a certain amount of shame involved.

- ■ **Fear that you've failed as a partner.** If you had been wiser, kinder, more loving, etc., maybe your partner wouldn't have left or you could have saved your marriage. This fear is compounded if your partner left you for someone else or decided that you weren't worth the effort. So, added to this is the fear of being unlovable.

- ■ **Fear of not being able to support yourself.** If you've been a stay-at-home parent or have limited resources, you may be terrified at the thought of retraining, finding a job, and supporting yourself.

- ■ **Fear of being able to function adequately as a single parent.** You may have already started to identify the many things your partner covered when it came to the kids—from providing lunch money, to teacher conferences, to carpooling. It can feel daunting to be responsible for all of this by yourself.

- ■ **Fear of losing your children's love**. You may fear that your kids won't love you as much as their other parent, or worse, fear they won't love you as much as the person your Ex is dating. The other parent may have financial resources that you do not, and it may feel as though he or she is buying the kids' affection. This fear is compounded when you feel your children are being alienated. The thought of losing our children rattles us to the core. You may fear the first holiday you will spend without your children.

■ **Fearing things outside your control.** There are many things you cannot control, especially when it comes to your children. You cannot control what happens in your children's lives when they are with their other parent. You cannot control who your former partner is dating or when and how those dates are introduced to the children. You can't control what your kids eat, when they go to bed, who they play with, or the type of medical care they receive when they aren't with you.

■ **Fears about how your divorce will impact your friendships.** Will they stop being your friends? Will they take sides? Will your friends (or family) tire of you talking about your divorce? Will they think you're unreasonable or out of control? Will they quit calling or answering the phone?

■ **Fear around how everything will get done.** Who will wash the windows, maintain the car, bring in the money, get the house ready for sale, walk the dog, get the kids to soccer practice, balance the checkbook, fix the computer? The list goes on and on.

Did you find some of your fears on that list? We usually have many, and they are the source of a lot of pain and confusion. Like all emotions, fear has a message. Healthy fear alerts us to a possible future event that could be harmful. For example, we know we aren't always going to be as spry as we are today, and being alone as we age can leave us vulnerable. Animals have a built-in fear that alerts them to predators. They prepare to fight or flee. We, on the other hand, have the ability to weigh the evidence and determine if our fear is founded. Unfortunately, we can also create such magnificent stories around our fears that they take on a life of their own. Often our fear is out of proportion to the actual danger. When we know this, we can put the fear into perspective. A supportive friend who is removed from the turmoil of it all can provide an objective perspective. We will talk more about ways to manage your thoughts later in the book.

Solution for Fear: Choosing Love

Think of as many emotions as you can, the good and bad, intense and calm, scary and beautiful, positive and negative, light and heavy. If you trace any given emotion to its common denominator, you will notice that each emotion is rooted in either love or fear. The lighter/higher emotions have their roots in love. The heavier/darker emotions are rooted in fear.

Fear cannot occupy the same space as love, just as light and darkness cannot occupy the same space. Walk into a darkened room, flip the light switch, and darkness disappears. Where does it go? It doesn't go anywhere. It didn't really exist as a thing of its own but is more like an absence, a non-thing. Flipping the switch allowed light to come in and fill the vacuum. Could fear also be a non-thing and be easily replaced by something as simple as bringing love to a situation? It often works that way.

Is focusing on the love/light side of life the same as faith? I'm not sure. One thing I do know is that having faith that things will turn out for the best is helpful. When we trust, we feel in touch with our own resources and are re-Sourced by something greater than ourselves that knows more about how life works than we do. Having that kind of trust reduces a lot of fear.

When we bring light to a fearful situation, that is, when we shine the light of our awareness onto the details, we see reality for what it is, and the fear begins to dissipate. We've exposed the boogie man, and, much like Oz, he's nothing but a small man behind a screen of smoke and mirrors.

Exploring Fear and Love

Here is a simple exercise: When you feel sad, angry, jealous, guilty, anxious, or any other "negative" emotion, ask yourself, "*What am I afraid of right now?*" Some common responses are fear of being rejected or replaced, fear that you are not good enough, that there isn't enough to go around, or that you won't be safe. When you are feeling good about things, ask yourself, "*What am I feeling love for right now?*" Perhaps someone did something special for you, or you got a promotion at work. You may find love in some interesting places.

As you begin to pay attention, you will note that love and fear feel quite different and have different impacts.

- Love: is expansive, thinks abundance, heals, stays connected, builds, releases, pursues.

- Fear: retracts inward, thinks scarcity, hurts, runs away, tears down, holds tightly, hides.

Notice how different you feel inside when you simply read each list. The list of loving qualities is peaceful and calming. The list of fearful characteristics is constricting and painful. Which would you rather experience? What would help you stay focused on the love side?

Above-the-Line Emotions

The difference between the loving qualities and the fearful ones can help you identify where you are in your own inner landscape. Emotions are a good gauge for determining where we spend the majority of our thought time. In the chart opposite, the emotions below the line are default reactions based in fear. They are weighty and often painful. The above-the-line emotions are peaceful, feel-good emotions of a higher frequency. We don't come by these emotions naturally. We are programmed to avoid pain over pursuing pleasure. It is not necessary to force yourself to think above-the-line thoughts; sometimes you just can't. If you're in pain, the appropriate response is to be with the pain, but when you can, choose the more positive emotions. Practicing in less intense moments will make it easier when the really tough stuff hits.

You will be referring to this chart several times throughout the book; you may want to bookmark it to find it easily.

Line Chart of Emotions

Love/Forgiveness
High Vibration

Conscious Choices

Acceptance—Trust—Prosperity—Abundance— Creation—We—Love—Learning—Gratitude—Integrity— True Vision—Happiness—Intentionality—Choice— Freedom—Celebration—Joy—Unity—Reflection—Living in the Present—Faith—Playfulness—Inclusion—Fairness—Enough— Pride—Respect—Excitement—Serenity—Security—Ease— Relaxation—Appreciation—Hope—Awareness— Calling Forth —Optimism—Contentment—Intimacy— Nurture—Sensuality—Worthiness—Equality— Praise—Embrace— Friendship—Self-worth

Default Reactions

Us/Them—Scarcity—Limits—Reaction—Accusation—Shame— Blame—Guilt—Betrayal—Resignation—Apathy—Complaints— Manipulation—Obsession—Resistance—Self-righteousness— Must—Should—Doubt—Win/Lose—Resentment— Brooding—Living in the Past/Future—Tolerance— Revenge—Jealousy—Hatred—Annoyance—Isolation— Confusion—Inadequacy—Embarrassment—Striving— Anxiety—Rejection—Depression—Inferior/Superior— Suspicion—Criticism—Sarcasm—Loneliness— Dominance—Perfectionism—Worthlessness

Fear/Non-Forgiveness
Low Vibration

Neutralizing Fear with Love

You can use the opposing qualities of love and fear for your benefit. Fear has power because we, well, fear it. When we find a way to love it instead, its grip lessens. (It's a little like inviting a cranky neighbor to your party, rather than excluding them. In the future you find the neighbor to be friendlier.) Resisting anything, including an emotion, just seems to make it stronger. Embracing it, on the other hand, takes the charge out of it and is another step toward wholeness.

Here is a simple exercise to help you do this.

Neutralizing Fear with Love[10]

■ Find an emotion below the line from which you would like relief. Then look above the line and find an emotion you would counteract it with. Use it to neutralize the painful emotion.

■ Use the sentence: I will meet _____ (fill in the blank with a lower emotion) with _____ (fill in the blank with a higher emotion).

For example: *"I will meet my fear with love."* Or *"I will meet my anger with compassion."* Fear often just wants attention, like a young child who is afraid. Embracing it with compassion, love, forgiveness, or any number of positive emotions can calm it down.

You can do this at any time with any of your emotions. Here's how it worked for Floyd: Suffering from a chronic feeling of inadequacy, Floyd was driven to perfectionism. He had to be the best employee, the best co-worker, the best provider, the best ball player on the team. There was no room for error in his world. When his wife had an affair, he felt that he'd failed at being the best husband; it was very painful. After learning about this idea, Floyd chose the following statement. *"I will embrace my inadequacy with acceptance."* At first, it was very difficult for him and he had to remind himself often, but after a while he was able to lighten up.

Questioning Fearful Thoughts

Overcoming fear begins with thinking about what you're thinking about. That is, observe your fearful beliefs from a little bit of a distance so you can question them instead of accepting them as reality. Are your thoughts running you, or are you running them? If your thoughts aren't serving you, you can change them. Being able to control your thoughts is an empowering and valuable life skill.

Even though there is an entire section in this book dedicated to changing your thinking, I include this exercise here for your immediate use as it speaks directly to fear.

Question Fearful Thoughts

The following steps, adapted from Byron Katie's book, *Loving What Is*, will help you question the validity of your thoughts. So many of our fears are imagined; following these steps can bring us back to reality.

- First, question the reality of the fear. Is your fear actually true, or are you making it up or magnifying it? Fear can cause us to blow things out of proportion. Take, for example, the belief *"I'm going to be left penniless from this divorce."* Is that true, or could it be an exaggeration?

- Next, think about how you would feel if you couldn't think such a thought. Allow the thought to disappear. It doesn't exist. It never existed. Perhaps you now have concern about your financial situation but can also see some options other than being penniless. There is nearly always a sense of relief and lightness when we give up our claim to a hurtful thought.

- And last, consider that the opposite might be true. *"I will keep my home. I will have a great job. I won't live under a bridge."* Or even a modified version: *"Even if I don't keep the same house, I will make wherever I am my home."* Or: *"If I lose my job, I'll find another one, maybe one that is a better fit for me."* Feel the difference? One way is empowering; the other is not. As long as you're making it up, why not make it up in a way that is more empowering?

Staying Present

Another key to managing fear is to live in the present moment. The past may be riddled with disappointments and regrets, and you may fear an unknown future, but right now, in this moment, how are things? Chances are that in this moment things are fine. And now, in this moment? Things are still fine. And in this moment, too. What about now? You just experienced four moments where things are just fine. Focusing on the present moment allows it to expand. With enough good moments in a row, pretty soon you've had an hour where things have been all right. Try to focus there.

It is common to think that fear is a sign that says, "Stop." Perhaps you want to try a new career, or a new relational behavior like telling someone "no", and then fear comes up. *"What if they never speak to me again?"* Too often we backtrack, taking fear as a sign that it was the wrong thing to do. There is a book called *Feel the Fear and Do It Anyway* by Susan Jeffers. It may be more useful to you a little later in your process, but the title sums it up. Fear doesn't have to be a stop sign; it may be a sign to proceed, albeit with caution.

Summary: Tips for Managing Fear

- Be aware of what you are thinking about. Don't let fear run unbridled.

- Write your story with a positive spin and a good ending. Choose love over fear.

- Neutralize difficult emotions with positive emotions.

- Live in the present moment where peace resides.

- Take positive action however and wherever you can.

- Realize that fear is a non-thing and only has the power that you give it.

- Find the center of the storm in whatever way works for you until you "know that you know" that, in some mysterious way, life is unfolding as it should, and you will have the resources to make the most of it.

Where Are You Now?

How are you at managing your fear?

I'm afraid for my very survival.

I have moments of sheer terror but am learning to question it.

I trust that I will get what I need. My fear is minimal.

13

Wrung with Worry

*Worrying is carrying tomorrow's load with today's
strength—carrying two days at once.
It is moving into tomorrow ahead of time.
Worrying doesn't empty tomorrow of its sorrow,
it empties today of its strength.*

— CORRIE TEN BOOM

The simple definition of worry is a preoccupation with events that have the potential to turn out badly. Worry bothers everyone at one time or another and can be a constant source of misery when going through a divorce or significant breakup.

Worry is often characterized by the phrases "If only . . ." and "What if . . ." "If only" thoughts occur when things are different than you wish they were. It can be as simple as, *"If only it hadn't rained"* or as complicated as *"If only my Ex would see things my way."* You may be prone to "if only" thoughts if you feel at the mercy of your circumstances or don't trust your ability to turn things around in a positive way.

"What if" is about the future: *"What if my Ex takes away my parenting time?"* *"What if I don't have enough money to live on?"* Sometimes we imagine a positive "what if," but more often we are asking "what if" to avoid something negative. It is natural to want to prepare ourselves. Asking "what if" can help us avoid future unpleasant realities.

There is nothing that causes worry quite like not having control over your circumstances. If you wanted the divorce, you may have had an idea in your head about how the divorce process would go. Your Ex would get X number of assets, and X time with the kids, and it would all be so simple. After all, you've thought it through and it makes perfect sense to you. But then your partner shows up with a completely different agenda.

- She wants half of that family inheritance you got a few years ago.
- You thought he would pay child support, but he plans to quit his job and let you pay him.
- She wants to go back to school and wants you to pay for it.
- He wants equal time with the kids, even though he never did before.

Of course you will worry about how things are going to turn out. There is a lot at stake.

Observing Worry

Like so many things, observing our tendency to worry helps us get some distance from it. Most of us don't realize how much we worry. We may feel that we worry all the time, or that we worry far less than we actually do. If you can develop a practice of catching a thought mid-worry, you can examine it and decide if it is worth all the effort you are giving it, or you can make a plan to do something about what is troubling you. It starts with keeping track.

Notice What You Worry About

Pay attention to the things that cause you to worry. On a piece of paper make three columns with the titles, Past, Future, Other. As you watch your thoughts, place a check in the categories as you notice the source of your worries. If it helps, make a simple note as a reminder. After you have done this for a week, look for trends. Are your thoughts more about the past or the future? What other things do you worry about?

Notice Triggering Events

If this is a useful exercise for you, you might want to start recording what you were thinking about when you started to worry. Were you triggered when you looked at the financial pages in the newspaper? After you dropped off the kids with your Ex? After hanging around with a certain doomsday friend? After you have tracked your triggers for a while, come back to these questions.

- Do you worry more or less at certain times (like at night) or during certain activities (like tending to financial matters)?

- Do certain people trigger your worries?
- What can you do to protect yourself from the things that trigger you?

Do a Reality Check

All worries need a reality check. A fearful mind can take on a life of its own, creating worries that are out of proportion to the situation. Here are some questions that might help.

- Is this worry realistic?
- What is the probability of it actually happening?
- If it does happen, how will I handle it?
- What can I do now to minimize any potential negative effects?
- What allies do I need? What resources should I seek?
- If it does happen, will the outcome matter in a year? Five years? Ten years?

Creating a Special Time to Worry

Some people find it helpful to have a designated place and time to worry. It provides a sort of on/off switch. Unlike grief, which will show up when it feels like it, worry can be managed with a little effort. When you have a designated time and place to worry you don't need to "worry things out" at every spare moment. You can stay more focused on your present tasks and tend to the worrisome thoughts at their given time.

Scheduling Worry

As much as you can, choose the same time and place each day. Choose a place that you don't otherwise frequent as you will soon come to associate this place with worry. Try a place in the basement, the back seat of your car, or a spot in the woods. To avoid taking your worries to bed, arrange your worry time to be earlier in the day when you will have more positive distractions afterward. Worrying at night may cost you much-needed sleep.

You can use your worry time to put your worries into three helpful categories:

- Things you can do something about

- Things you can influence but not control

- Things that are outside your control and which you can do nothing about

After you've done this, consider the wisdom of the Dalai Lama: "If you have fear of some pain or suffering, you should examine whether there is anything you can do about it. If you can, there is no need to worry about it; if you cannot do anything, then there is also no need to worry."

Practicing Presence as
a Solution for Worry

The wise encourage us to accept any situation as though we had purposely chosen it. Why? Because it empowers us. *"Like it or not, this is my current life situation. What shall I do with it?"* When we completely accept what is, we have the power to change it. If we don't grasp the opportunity, we are little more than powerless victims. The powerful path is to always take charge of what we can. When you shut the door on the past and stop viewing the future as either a savior or a villain, it is the stillness of this moment where things are okay that remains. Taking action from that sense of peace is far more powerful than making decisions from fear or reactivity.

Where Are You Now?

What is your approach to worry?

I worry far more
than I want.

I worry very little. I
trust that all will be
well in the end.

Worry gets the better of
me sometimes but I am
beginning to have confidence
in myself and my future.

14

Crushing Rejection

*I take rejection as someone blowing a bugle in my ear
to wake me up and get going, rather than retreat.*

— SYLVESTER STALLONE

When someone leaves us, it is very painful, especially if we didn't see it coming. Perhaps you thought things were just fine in your relationship. Maybe you knew things weren't perfect, but didn't think they were serious enough to divorce over. Maybe your former partner left you for someone else, which is perhaps the greatest rejection. It is common to feel deep hurt, despair, frustration, and intense anger after being rejected. Since being accepted by others is a vital human need, it is understandable that being rejected has the potential to unravel us.

Partners leave us in more ways than just physically— and often before the marriage ends. Maybe your partner was a workaholic; had a chemical dependency or a mental or physical illness; or was more interested in pornography, him or herself, or another person. All these things can leave us without a partner present. If your attempts to call your partner back to relationship failed, it is likely that the feelings of rejection grew. It's hard to have someone you love actively choose something or someone ahead of you.

Rejection isn't exclusive to divorce. Even common events like being fired from a job, having a child leave home (empty nest), being deployed or taking a long-distance job, or the memory loss of an aging parent can leave us feeling alone.

Rejection and Self-Worth

We experience the pain of rejection to the degree that we allow others to determine our worth. Many of us relied on our partners to help us feel good about ourselves. When the assurance was there we felt okay, but when it stopped, our sense of well-being vanished. We may feel untethered, unlovable, and lose sight of who we are. Maybe you tried to be what your partner wanted so she wouldn't leave you. If that works at all, it is only temporary because that isn't the solution. You can turn yourself inside out trying to become what she wants and it still won't satisfy her. What she craves must be found inside, not outside, herself. This works the same way for men, of course. You can only be true to yourself, and rearranging yourself according to someone else's need never works.

When you have a stronger sense of self you will realize that relationships end, and that rejection is part of adult life. While still painful, it doesn't have to be devastating. You can learn from it and move on. As you identify the dynamics that contributed to the end of your relationship, which we will do later in the book, you will find that you were not the only "problem" in the relationship, and that will help lessen the feelings of rejection.

Managing Rejection

You are valuable. Just because your former partner no longer seems to appreciate your gifts and strengths doesn't mean you don't have them. Focusing on your strengths will help you recover your temporarily lost self-worth. You may even develop a sense of pity for your former partner because he or she is missing out on being with you.

It can help to remember that your partner may, in fact, appreciate much about you. Leaving a relationship may be precipitated by reasons that have nothing to do with you, e.g., midlife crisis, differing life paths, or a change of sexual orientation. Your partner may leave relationship with you because he or she needs something different. That "different" is not necessarily better. Just different. Knowing this may help the Heartbroken with feelings of rejection, and the Heartbreaker with feelings of guilt. Sometimes, we choose to leave a job or profession that we still really appreciate and care about because something different is calling us. This can happen in relationship, too. We are changing individuals living in a fast-paced world. It is more and more common to go through several careers, more than one marriage, and even several identities as we keep outgrowing current versions of self. Life is change, and having a partner decide to move on is not necessarily an indictment of you, though it sure can feel that way.

Help for Managing Rejection

Think of one of your most important strengths, and yes, you do have them. (You don't want to dismiss your strengths and inadvertently participate in *self*-rejection!) For ten minutes give yourself permission to be over-the-top positive about this characteristic. Instead of, *"I am okay,"* try saying, *"I am super-duper smart, creative and intelligent, playful and fun, too. I'm getting better with every breath. It's a blast to be so awesome."* It helps to write it down. Or speak it into a mirror. Write it as though you believe it is true in this moment. Do it even if it feels like you're telling yourself outrageous, self-glorifying, bold-faced lies. Go ahead. No one is watching!

How does it feel to let yourself have such a bold rant? It's good to speak positively about yourself.

Where Are You Now?

What is your level of self-rejection?

My lover no longer wants me. How can I not feel rejected? I'm experiencing tremendous pain.

I don't need my Ex to remind me I'm awesome. I know it for myself!

I know the solution for rejection is to create an awesome life and reclaim my self-image. I'm taking those steps.

15

The Ache of Loneliness

Nothing ever goes away until it has
taught us what we need to know.

— PEMA CHÖDRÖN

Loneliness is a painful emotion. It makes you ache. Loneliness is one of the most difficult emotions to endure and one of the most common byproducts of breakup and divorce.

You can, of course, also be lonely in relationship. People have told me that is often where they were the most lonely. With a partner we, by all rights, should have felt emotionally met, but often we did not. And that was heartbreaking. Once the marriage actually dissolves, it sets the stage for a new kind of loneliness to set in.

Loneliness is not just the state of being alone; it's the feeling that we *are* alone; sometimes we feel we are the only ones who have ever experienced such depravity of the heart. It is the feeling of missing something, of missing connection, of being turned inside out and finding nothing there. Nothing makes us feel quite so alone as engaging in activities once shared with another, or the quiet of our empty home once filled with lively chatter. Fifteen trips to the refrigerator doesn't quiet that kind of loneliness.

The Need to Connect

The message of loneliness is that we need to connect. Yes, you need to connect with others, but more importantly, you need to connect with yourself. If you were married a long time or in an entangled relationship, or even if your life has had many demands, you've probably lost touch with who you are, what you enjoy, what you would do with your spare time if no one objected.

We can feel terribly alone even when surrounded by people if we keep our emotions, ideas, and interests to ourselves. You may have been lonely in your marriage because you were unwilling or unable to freely share yourself. Maybe your partner didn't want to hear or wasn't safe to share with, but often it is more about our own inability to connect deeply. We are not practiced at saying things like, *"I need you to listen."*

Where Loneliness Begins

The ways we did, or did not, connect to our earliest caregivers has a lifelong impact, especially when it comes to the depth of our feelings of loneliness. Have you asked yourself questions like: Why do I long for closeness? Why do I feel panicked when my partner leaves me? Why is hard for me to be vulnerable and show my true self? Why do I want to just take care of myself rather than depend on others? Many of our basic relational difficulties *and* strengths stem from the ways we did or did not connect to our primary caretakers.

Ideally we develop a loving bond with our early caregivers, and that paves the way for a lifetime of good relating. Learning basic trust to be emotionally responsive, to feel good about ourselves, and to feel safe in our relationships helps us cope with the stresses of marriage later in life. It allows us to come to marriage with our love tank filled.

A lack of emotional connection leads to a feeling of emptiness. There is an emotional hunger that is satisfied only by intimacy. I like this definition of intimacy: *in-to-me-see*. We have a primal need to be known. How we deal with this need varies, if we even allow ourselves to feel it.

Those who had an emotionally absent caregiver may have special challenges in life and in marriage. The effects are especially applicable to feelings of loneliness.[11]

These include:

- Holes in your sense of value and self-esteem
- Difficulty taking in love and establishing intimate relationships
- Feeling undernourished and emotionally starved
- Loneliness and feelings of not belonging
- Feeling as if you don't have enough support
- Difficulty accepting and advocating for your needs

- Not knowing how to process feelings
- Pervasive sense of scarcity
- Sense of struggle
- Depression
- Addictive behaviors
- Perfectionism and self-criticism
- Difficulty finding your authentic voice and following your passion

Although I don't see it very often, there are some who come to marriage, and subsequently divorce, with a pervasive sense of lack. They experience near terror while divorcing because the separation brings up early abandonment feelings. It feels more like an infant separating from a caregiver than one adult separating from another. If you are having this experience, I encourage you to seek therapeutic help. While it may seem so, it doesn't have to be a life sentence. Please don't give up. It's all part of your personal development.

Finding Intimacy

In order to be known, we must reveal ourselves to other people. This can be frightening. We feel so vulnerable when we are going through a divorce or major breakup, and to risk reaching out and opening up can be terrifying. We could be rejected, misunderstood, or ridiculed. Perhaps we believe, *"If they really knew me, they wouldn't want to be around me."* While those are possibilities, it is still true that the way to appease loneliness is human connection.

Remember that in order to have "different," you must do "different." The risk of reaching out is often the first growth step we face when getting back into life, and many of us don't feel up to it. It is, however, an important ingredient for completing the second turning point.

Sexual Intimacy?

Many people equate sexual intimacy with relational intimacy, believing that if they are having sex, they are experiencing intimacy. While it takes some risk to be sexually intimate, it takes more risk to reveal one's heart. As too many people have found, sexual intimacy does little to ease long-term loneliness. A lasting solution is to share the deeper parts of yourself in safe, non-sexual relationships: that is, with people who love all of you without expecting anything in return. Take a moment to identify the people you have grown closer to since the dissolution of your relationship—those who listen without judging, who are there for you in your worst moments. Those are the intimate friends with whom it is safe to share. Invest in these friendships and loneliness will begin to subside.

Healthy Aloneness

Some of us went from our childhood home to living with a roommate to cohabiting and never learned how to be alone. A period of healthy aloneness is a worthwhile goal when leaving a long-term relationship. If you've never lived alone, that is an important next step. A time of solitude, when you can be completely alone and learn about yourself, is an important part of your personal development during and after divorce. It will help you develop an inner sense of self, identify your weaknesses and strengths, allow you to get to know who you are without the influence of other people, especially your former partner. I encourage you to be on your own for a while—at least a year, preferably two, to develop a sense of wholeness, to become your own ally, and to get acquainted with yourself again. Aloneness is inherent to human life. We may have wonderful people who walk alongside us in this life, but when they go home or they go to sleep, there we are again—with ourselves. Being happy with our own company is the only lasting solution to loneliness. Learning to enjoy your own company is an important aspect of the fourth turning point.

The Aloneness Query

The biggest gift of being alone is the freedom to do what you want to do. If you want to play the stereo LOUD at 3:00 a.m. or take off for the weekend, you can. You don't have to consider someone else. It may be disconcerting at first to make decisions about what *you* alone want to do without consulting others, but you will grow to appreciate the freedom in it.

A period of aloneness allows you the freedom to do some personal exploration.

- What hobby do I want to take up?
- Which new instrument appeals to me?
- What sport am I attracted to?
- What club do I want to join?
- Do I want to stay home tonight and read a book, or do I want to go out with friends?

When you choose what you want to do, like stay home and read on a Friday night instead of feeling compelled by loneliness to go out to look for romance, you will know you've created a healthy aloneness.

Obstacles to Connecting

Some of the loneliness we feel is a natural result of losing our partner and the life we've been used to. Some is the result of walls we build around our hearts so that even when we're with others we don't share in a way that allows us to feel connected. The questions below will help you explore those walls. Maybe there are some walls you no longer need.

Complete these sentences quickly, with the first thing that comes to mind:

- When I think of getting close to someone again, I feel _____.
- When I think about reaching out to someone, I _____.

- When I think of new people I might like or when I meet people I could potentially have a friendship with, I notice _____.
- When I start to feel lonely, I _____.

What did you notice as you answered these questions? Did you identify some fears? Some protective strategies? Sometimes, when our loneliness grows too strong, it is actually harder to reach out because we are more overwhelmed by difficult feelings and a negative self-image. Reaching out before we get to this point is helpful.

Ideally we want to be able to connect and also to be alone. Most of us haven't mastered this balance. We either don't connect as comfortably or intimately as we might like or we are a bit compulsive about connecting and can't stand to be alone. On the scale below, mark where you are between the two extremes. Do you like where you are? What can you do to move more toward the center ideal range?

Where Are You Now?

Where are you on the loneliness scale?

I don't need or want to connect.

Ideal Range = Able to connect and to be alone.

I feel emotionally needy.

Part Four

MANAGING YOUR THOUGHTS

16

Choosing Your Interpretations

*A man's mind may be likened to a garden which may
be intelligently cultivated or allowed to run wild.
Just as a gardener cultivates his plot, keeping it free
from weeds and growing the flowers and fruits he
requires, so may a man tend the garden of his mind,
weeding out all the wrong, useless, and impure
thoughts, and cultivating toward perfection the flowers
and fruits of right, useful, and pure thoughts.*

— JAMES ALLEN, *AS A MAN THINKETH*

Have you ever jumped to a conclusion or misinterpreted a comment spoken to you, only to find out later you were completely wrong? Everyone has had that experience. Have you taken a smallish setback in your divorce only to have your mind turn it into a doomsday fear? That happens a lot, too. Sometimes our thinking is like a runaway horse. Once loose it may be nearly impossible to corral, and yet, if you want some peace, you must. Calming your thoughts is an important part of the second turning point.

If I could teach you only one skill to help you through your divorce it would be the skill of managing your thinking.

The majority of the pain we experience throughout life, and the majority of pain we experience in our divorce, is due to the way we think about the things that happen. Events are just things—neutral things. A stoplight is a thing. If you have an hour to spare on your way to a friend's house you probably don't care about a red light all that much. If you're on your way to the hospital for an emergency, that stoplight is going to matter a lot. Thoughts can be positive and productive or limiting and defeating. They can bring us to new vistas or keep us stuck. If you decide something is negative, it will be.

We may not get to choose the thoughts that appear in our minds or the things that happen to us. Sometimes they just come as they want. But we do have control over the meaning we assign to the things that happen to us. This is key. Once you understand this, it will set you free.

So the next time you get an email from your Ex, observe what your mind does. Do you immediately feel anxious? Are you afraid of what it might say? Are you curious? Are you happy? Would you like it to feel better, or at least different? There are a number of steps along the way to feeling good or feeling bad. When you know what they are, you will be able to intervene at several points along the way for a more positive outcome.

The Process of Interpretation

First, here's an overview of the steps, then I will explain them in more detail.

An **Event** (email, phone ringing, knock on the door) is viewed through your

> **lens** of understanding (or frame of mind), where it is immediately
>> **interpreted** (you make up a story about it), which elicits an
>>> **emotional response**, which leads to a
>>>> **behavior**, which leads to a
>>>>> **self-assessment** of being either okay or not okay

This chain of interpretation gives you a sense of hope, or hopelessness, depending on your initial interpretation. Below is an expansion of each of the steps.

The Event

An event is just a thing—like a sandwich or a toy truck. Maybe it's an unknown email, a phone call in the middle of the night, or an unexpected knock at the front door. Events remain neutral until we ascribe meaning to them.

We naturally view events through our personal lens. We have no choice; it is how we view our world.

Your Lens

Each of us looks at the world through the lenses we've developed from our various life experiences. We've all heard of the glass half full or the glass half empty. Your lens may cause you to view life as a playground or a haunted house, depending on your experiences. These lenses influence the way you view yourself and the world around you—the way you express yourself, explain yourself, deal with your past, and anticipate your future, but what you see may not reflect reality. Knowing your lens may be distorted helps you to know your view of reality may be incorrect. You can say, for example, *"I know I can be pessimistic. Is that influencing the way I am seeing this?"*

After viewing the event through your personal lens, you will immediately make an assessment and interpret the event.

The Interpretation

Your interpretation is how you view the event, the people involved, and yourself. Interpretations are ultimately either positive: hopeful, good, happy, etc.; or negative: discouraging, bad, sad, etc. Most of the time our interpretations are not based on fact. We simply don't know.

The interpretation we choose then elicits an emotional response.

The Emotional Response

If your interpretation is positive, you will experience joy, happiness, excitement, and the like. If your interpretation is negative, the resulting emotions may be sadness, anger, guilt, shame, anxiety, or fear.

Recognizing your emotional response is your second point of entry for changing the outcome. *"I'm feeling sad."* *"Oh, that's why. I wonder if I could shift my view?"*

Your emotional response will then trigger an action or behavior on your part.

The Behaviors

Behaviors follow emotions. If you're sad, you may cry. If you're mad, you may pound your fist. If you are happy, you might make special plans to celebrate. If you feel rejected, you may hide away. Your third point of entry for changing to a more positive outcome is to observe your behaviors. *"Wow, why am I behaving like this? I don't like being that way. I think I'll stop."*

The outcome of these steps lead to judgment about yourself—your value, your safety, your wisdom, and other things.

The Self-Judgment

Lightning quick, before you're even aware of it, you've come to the conclusion that you are either okay or not okay, depending on how you've interpreted the initial event. Maybe you don't think of it in terms of okay and not okay, perhaps you just become aware of a sense of doom, or apprehension, or other underlying pervasive emotion. It could be a positive emotion, too, of course, if you've interpreted the original event in a positive way.

Choosing Your Interpretation

It is my observation that when it comes to interpreting a situation positively or negatively, most of us naturally gravitate toward the negative. Perhaps anticipating a negative outcome prepares us in some way. I've not yet met a person who naturally believes the best all the time without having done considerable introspective work and self-observation. Learning this skill might be the best reason yet to do that work.

Let's apply these steps to a relational event. Perhaps a friend doesn't return your call. One scenario might go like this:

Event with a Negative Filter

Event: Friend didn't return my call.

(**Filter:** My history tells me friends go away and don't come back.)

Interpretation: S/he hates me.

Emotion: Loss/sadness/rejection

Behavior: Never call that friend again.

Result: Friendship ends or changes due to neglect.

Assessment: I'm not okay. I'll never have any friends.

Event with a Positive Filter

The same scenario, with a different filter, might look like this:

Event: Friend didn't return my call.

(**Filter:** My history tells me friends stick around and care about me. They think about me even when they are not immediately available.)

Interpretation: Something important must have come up.

Emotion: Disappointment about not hearing back; concern about friend's well-being; happy to have a good friend.

Behavior: Leave a message with encouraging words.

Result: Friendship continues and perhaps deepens
due to care shown.

Assessment: I'm okay. I have great friends.

The difference is striking. It all begins with the interpretation as seen through your unique filter. Have you experienced events in your divorce that left you feeling angry or confused and ultimately not okay? Once you become aware of how you end up there, you at least have a choice. You have the opportunity to choose a different interpretation for a different result.

Three Alternate Interpretations:

Because it is so easy to interpret things negatively, it is helpful to train yourself to purposely make up three positive interpretations as alternatives to your default—three interpretations that lead to an "I'm okay" conclusion.

Three potential alternate interpretations to the scenario just described could be:

- Friend's Mom/dog/child is in the hospital, and s/he wasn't able to call. (leads to compassion)
- Friend is planning a surprise party for me and doesn't want to tip me off. (leads to joy, gratitude)
- Friend has laryngitis. (leads to empathy)

It is important to allow your alternate interpretations to be just as real to you as your default. As funny as it sounds, it's all made up anyway! You might as well make it up in a way that makes you feel good about yourself. And, of course, check in with your friend at some point to find out what actually happened.

Alternate interpretations to believing your Ex isn't going to cooperate might be s/he was tired during the mediation, s/he was thinking about the impact to his or her own life, s/he needed some time to think about other options. There could be dozens of interpretations that aren't about you at all. It is human nature to take things personally, but it doesn't usually help and is often not true.

You can change your thinking any time your interpretations are making you miserable. Remember that we do much of this to ourselves! Divorce happens, but much of the drama is self-inflicted. Now that you know how your interpretations lead to happiness or misery, you can gain some control over them. The blank template on the next page is provided for your use. Start by identifying some of your possible lenses/filters.

How Are You Doing?

How are you at thinking positively?

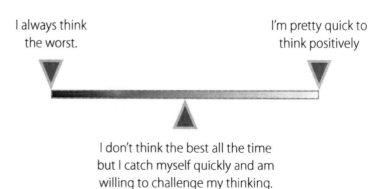

I always think
the worst.

I'm pretty quick to
think positively

I don't think the best all the time
but I catch myself quickly and am
willing to challenge my thinking.

Process of Interpretation Tool

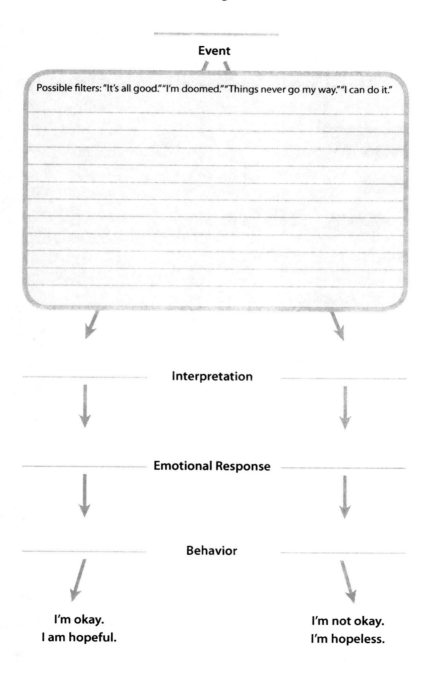

Event

Possible filters: "It's all good." "I'm doomed." "Things never go my way." "I can do it."

Interpretation

Emotional Response

Behavior

I'm okay.   I'm not okay.
I am hopeful.   I'm hopeless.

Changing Hurtful Beliefs

Experience is not what happens to you.
Experience is what you do with what happens to you.

— ALDOUS HUXLEY

If you were told as a child that you wouldn't amount to anything, chances are you believed it on some level. Maybe you still do. Maybe your Ex is saying similar things to you, and your self-image is low enough that you believe him or her. Many of our deeply held beliefs were drawn during childhood when our self-image was still being formed. If your parents seemed rejecting, for example, you may have believed something was wrong with you. As a child, you didn't know that they were overwhelmed with other things, you only knew they weren't there with you. So, in essence, before you knew it wasn't about you, you had already developed hurtful beliefs about yourself. If you brought a poor self-image to your marriage, you likely found plenty of evidence in your partner's attitude or comments that confirmed it. Bringing a poor self-image to divorce creates a platform for other negative experiences to attach to throughout the process, causing further hurt.

Our beliefs attract evidence like magnets. If you believe that you are unlovable, you will find plenty of evidence to support that. If you believe that you are not worth half of the assets accumulated during your marriage, you will, without outside help to change that thinking, find evidence that confirms that belief. Have you ever noticed how people who believe they are beautiful, are, inside and out?

It is good practice to question your beliefs. I like the bumper sticker that reads: *Don't believe everything you think.* It's a good goal. Some beliefs are good and worth keeping. Many are not.

Identifying Hurtful Beliefs

Below is a list of a few common, hurtful, beliefs divorcing people often hold.[12] Put an **X** by any you feel are true for you. These are just examples. Change them so they fit for you. Be sure to add others that apply to you.

Beliefs about your Ex:

____ If I ask for what I want, my Ex will just make things harder.

____ If I don't take control, I will be hurt/taken advantage of.

____ What's the use? My Ex always gets his/her way.

____ Everybody (your choice: mediator, friends, kids, in-laws, lawyer, God) is on my Ex's side.

Beliefs about yourself:

_____ I will never be able to put my life back together.

_____ If only I would (or wouldn't) have _____ we could still be together.

_____ I am a bad parent/person for _____ (breaking up the family, crying too much, being angry, letting this happen, etc.)

_____ I am hurting the ones I love.

_____ I don't deserve to be happy.

_____ I'm not _____ (attractive, successful, young, rich, happy, etc.) enough.

_____ I'm too _____ (old, ugly, dysfunctional, poor, stupid, emotional, etc.).

_____ I will be alone forever.

_____ I'm sinful.

What else?

Once you start identifying your (often unknown) beliefs, you may be surprised at the length of your list. It is illuminating to get these beliefs out of your head and onto paper where you can look at them. They are often so subtle and/or familiar that it is easy to forget that THEY ARE NOT YOU! If they are not you, you can ignore them, change them, or dance on their little heads. It doesn't matter.

We develop our beliefs over time from the way we relate to our many life experiences. We believe they are true because we've experienced them, but experience doesn't always translate to truth, as we saw in the last chapter. A belief is a story we've told ourselves for so long that it's become real. *"The world is round." "I am fat." "People love me."* It serves us to test our beliefs, keep the ones that serve, and let go of the rest.

Unfortunately, when we merely toss a belief aside, it has a way of finding its way back home. There is a lot of energy behind our beliefs. To effectively leave them behind they will need a little dismantling. The exercises below will help tease apart your hurtful beliefs, uproot them, and replace them with something more empowering.

Replacing Hurtful Beliefs with Empowering Beliefs

Choose one of your most hurtful beliefs. By way of example, I will use the belief that divorcing people are losers. Perhaps this is one of yours.

Next, identify the reasons you hold your belief. A little archaeological digging may be just the thing to help you let it go. Use the questions below. I've provided some possible responses for this particular belief.

Here are the questions:

1. Why do you have this belief? Where did it come from?

2. How has this belief served you?

3. How has it limited you?

4. How would things be for you without this belief?

1. **Why do you have this belief?** Where did it come from? Example: "I remember when my neighbor went through a divorce, she was a basket case. All she could talk about was her how her husband was screwing her. Nobody wanted to be around her. She just couldn't get her act together."

2. **How has this belief served you?** "If I saw her as crazy, I felt okay just ignoring her. I felt better about myself knowing I wasn't a loser like her. And I certainly didn't want to end up like her, so I worked like heck to keep my marriage together."

3. **How has this belief limited you?** "Now I'm divorcing. I cry every night because now I'm the loser."

4. **How would things be for you without this belief?** "I guess I could accept myself. If I wasn't a loser, I guess I'd have to be something else, like maybe just hurting."

- Now, re-write your belief in a way that is more empowering. You can do this by changing it to its opposite. Instead of "Divorcing people are losers," "Divorcing people are courageous."

- If you feel adventurous add a "because" phrase. "Divorcing people are courageous because _____."

You will want to takes steps to incorporate your new belief. Maybe you've heard the phrase, "To believe it is to be-live it." Make it part of your life. Declare your new way of thinking at every opportunity. Say it out loud. Meditate on it. Remind yourself of it each morning. Write it on an index card and attach it to the mirror. Bring it to mind every night before sleep. Take some time to picture yourself as a divorced person who has great courage. Better yet, change it just a little more to, "I am courageous because _____!" Make your new belief as real as you allowed the false belief to be. As you go about your day, look for evidence that confirms your new belief. Listen for it in the words of friends, family, and colleagues. Know that the book you've randomly picked off the shelf or the song you haven't heard in years is speaking directly to you when it talks about courage. The evidence is everywhere when you look.

You didn't develop your beliefs overnight and you won't change them overnight. Your outlook will shift over time. Changing a belief is a little like clearing a glass of murky water by adding one droplet of clear water at a time. When enough droplets have been added, the glass will be filled with clear water.

5. **The last question I want you to ask yourself is, "What would Love say about this belief?"** How about, "You'll get through this and be stronger for it. You're doing everything you know to do. It is enough. Be at peace."

Affirmations

Affirmations are another good way to shift hurtful beliefs to empowering beliefs. Our self-talk can be quite negative. We are often our own worst critic. Affirmations help us learn to speak kindly to ourselves, much as a nurturing parent or friend would speak to us, or the way we would speak to a young child who is trying to figure things out. Affirmations are a way to give your mind a second opinion and a new possibility. Affirmations challenge your default way of thinking. They help you recognize and acknowledge your gifts and strengths.

Affirmations work on a subconscious level. They aren't about trying to convince an unbelieving you of something that seems far-fetched. You don't have to believe them, and many times you won't, in order for them to work. You are just interjecting something new into your default way of thinking.

To be most effective, affirmations should be stated in the positive and in the present tense: *"I have . . ." "I am . . ."* Repeat an affirmation any time you want to change your thinking, such as when you wake up in the morning and that black cloud is hanging over you, or when you've had a difficult encounter related to your divorce, or with someone at work. Bring affirming words to mind when you find yourself in a funk and don't know why. Chances are you've had a default subconscious thought take you down the *"I'm not okay"* path without your being aware of it. Before sleep is also a great time. Don't worry if you fall asleep mid-sentence. It doesn't matter. What a great way to go to sleep!

Using Affirmations

You created a very specific affirmation for yourself by reversing your hurtful belief above. You can also use positive statements as an affirmation. What strengths do people say you have? I keep positive emails and phone messages that I can refer to at times when I'm feeling low. If you are part of an affirming spiritual tradition, it will be especially meaningful to use words from your own tradition that empower you.

Below is a list of ready-made affirmations for your use. Your goal is to repeat a chosen affirmation at key times throughout your day, preferably for a minimum of a week. If after that time your chosen affirmation has served its purpose, select a new one that feels right. Take advantage of this opportunity to speak kindly to yourself. Affirmations are a good way to remind you of the truth of who you are.

Use painful emotions as a signal to bring you back to the present moment by choosing an affirmation that refutes the false belief that took you out of the moment in the first place. For example, if you can't stop thinking about how you won't have enough money to survive, you might adopt any of these affirmations: *"I handle the events of my life with grace and ease." "I believe in myself."* Or *"I have exactly what it takes to improve my financial picture today."* Remember, affirmations are not about trying to convince yourself; they interject new possibilities into your habitual way of thinking. If you are diligent in practicing this nurturing form of self-talk, you will, after a while, detect a shift in your outlook.

List of Affirmations

I think the very best of myself in
all situations, at all times.

I believe in my ability to
achieve my goals.

I'd rather be me than anyone else.

I love life, and my life reflects that.

I am equal to whatever life hands me.

I find endless inspiration
all around me.

I give my best in everything I do.

I see the best in others.

I am prepared for success today.

I am improving my financial
picture today.

I have forgiveness for myself
and others.

All is well with me in this moment.

I believe in myself.

I have many things for which
to be thankful.

I am courageous.

I am worth my weight in gold.

I am a good friend to others.

I know that I am truly good.

I have an understanding of my
unique place in the Universe.

I contend with no one, argue with
no one. My highest self knows
what to do and when to do it.

I am free from the fear of
poverty, bondage, and any
thought of limitation.

I trust my inner guidance and wisdom.

The opportunity for self-expression
is always open to me.

My future is certain. I am free
from all fears of my past.

I live each moment in the
eternal present which is
filled only with good.

Happiness and wholeness fill
my entire being with the
realization that all is well.

My life experiences are leading
me to truth and love.

I handle the events of my life
with grace and ease.

I love, trust, and accept myself.

I am fun, friendly, and cheerful.

I am secure in who I am.

Everyone I meet loves me and
recognizes my worth.

I have meaningful work
that I'm good at.

I am in control of my destiny.

I accept myself just the way I am.

There is a divine plan of
goodness for me.

Life is richly rewarding to me.

I am gentle with myself and others.

I live my life in balance and harmony.

I respect others, and they respect me.

I have an abundance of good
things in my life.

I am a sensitive, caring individual.

My life is unfolding just as it should.

For more affirmations and a look at how you can change physical illness by "wording your world" in a different way, read *Heal Your Body* by Louise Hay.

Where Are You Now?

Where are you most of the time on the scale of hurtful to empowering beliefs?

My thoughts run me
most of the time.

I choose my
thoughts well.

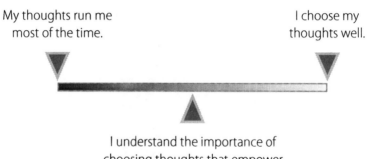

I understand the importance of
choosing thoughts that empower
me, and I'm working at it.

18

Taming Your Inner Critic

If my heart could do my thinking, and my head began to feel; would I look upon the world anew and know what's truly real?

— VAN MORRISON

D o you have a rascal voice in your head that just won't shut up? Does it speak at the most inopportune times and say hurtful things that cause you to feel like the lowest of scum? You're not alone. This is the voice of your inner critic, sometimes referred to as an inner judge. Everyone has one, usually several. Some are worse than others. All need to be tamed if we want to have a peaceful thought life. Originally designed to be a helpful guide, the inner critic has lost its way and become a critical nag instead. It is an extension of the ego—your false self. It runs rampant during a divorce, adding more pain to an already painful situation.

One of the reasons we feel so special when "falling in love" is it is one of the rare times our critic is quiet. It can't compete with all the positivity coming in from new love. Its voice is drowned in the sea of positivity. We know that doesn't last, however. The critic eventually returns. And when love is in short supply, as during divorce, the critic is merciless.

The critic believes it is keeping you safe. You could call it simply an inner protector if it weren't so . . . well . . . critical. When you were little, it said things like, "Wear your sweater when you go out." When you got a little older it said things like, "That was a stupid thing to say." Its thinking is that if it can yell at you first, maybe you'll take action before a real person says those awful things to you. Perhaps now your critic is telling you that you shouldn't get divorced, or that you're hurting your former mate or ruining your children. Nothing is off limits to its critique—not your parenting, your sexuality, your financial prowess, your intelligence, your body image, or your ways of relating.

The Critic is programmed to keep track and uphold "the rules"—your rules, your parents' rules, society's rules, any rule that might affect you. The more rules you have, the more attacks you will experience from your critic. This is one of the reasons it is wise to pay attention to the "shoulds" you put on yourself. *"I should be doing this. I shouldn't be doing that."* You could call it your conscience on steroids (remember Jiminy Cricket from *Pinocchio?*).

It will use the voice of any authority figure—a parent, teacher, older sibling, coach, pastor, or even a peer or celebrity you admire—to keep you in line. If you've viewed your Ex as a parent figure, it may use his or her voice, too. One of its main tools is guilt. An interesting exercise is to ask, *"Who does this sound like?"* When you recognize that the voice is not your own, you begin to have some power over it.

It can be devastating to live with a harsh inner critic. Fortunately, there is hope for taming it. It may continue to blather on, but you don't need to be controlled by it, and sometimes it fades considerably.

Before we go on to taming the inner critic, here is a quiz that will help you identify just how much the critic is running things.[13]

Rating Your Inner Critic

Rate the following on a three-point scale using the following:

I don't do this or do it very rarely: 0

I am somewhat like this: 1

I am often like this: 2

___I'm concerned about what others think of me.

___I replay conversations over and over and beat myself up for things I've said.

___I need more: education, looks, money, savvy, so others will like me.

___I wish I was more attractive/likable/lovable.

___I compare myself to others.

___I'm convinced there is something fundamentally wrong with me.

___I can't say 'No' without feeling guilty.

___I believe that my decisions are wrong, no matter what I choose.

___I don't like to try new things because I might
fail or make a fool of myself.

___I can't ever seem to get it right.

___When I look in a mirror, I see only the flaws.

___I believe that if people really knew me, they
wouldn't like me.

___I feel that no matter how hard I try I'll never
be enough.

___I often wish I could do or say things over again
to get it right.

___Just about anyone knows how to do life better
than I do.

Scale:

0–5   Excellent! You are free to be your own person.

6–10   The critic is probably a small, manageable nuisance
in your life.

11–16 Your critic probably stymies you at important
junctures, perhaps keeping you frozen in old
patterns.

17–30 Your critic is a major block to your self-esteem.

How did you do with the quiz? It's not unusual to have
a disabling critic, especially while divorcing. It's trying so
hard to keep you safe, and safety is hard to come by. That
makes it cranky.

Since the critic is an extension of the ego, it is futile to
try to outsmart it, please it, argue, or reason with it. It will
wiggle right around any of those approaches. The critic has

an exaggerated sense of importance, is highly invested in protecting itself, and is not easily dismissed.

So what can we do with such an elusive but powerful enemy? The first thing to do is insert space between you and your critic.

Separating from the Critic

Start by noticing. Everything you notice about the critic helps you separate from it. When you are separate from it you realize it is not you. Separating from the critic is like noticing the technical aspects of a movie. You're not so sucked in that you forget that it is a movie. You can separate from the critic when you watch for the moves it makes and the words it uses. You're on alert. You further separate when you get curious about its motives rather than get caught up in what it is saying. What is it trying to protect you from? After a while, you will be able to spot potential attacks more readily, and the instances where your critic unexpectedly appears will decrease.

The important thing to remember is that you are the prime mover in your life—not your critic. You get to decide what is true for you. As a friend once said to me, "It's *your* head. You get to decide who lives there."

Observing the Critic

Part One: Over several days or even weeks, notice what your inner critic tells you. As much as possible, just note it without trying to make sense of it or analyzing it.

What does your inner critic tell you about:

- How you look
- Your ability to get beyond your breakup or divorce
- How you act toward your former partner
- Your sexuality
- Your desirability as a future romantic partner
- Your health/physical prowess/athletic ability
- How you take care of yourself
- Divorcing at the age you are
- Your ability to find work or create income
- Your ability to make and keep friends?
- What else does it tell you?

Part Two: Next, acknowledge what the critic has said, but choose what *you* want to believe and how *you* want to act. For instance, you have the thought *"I look fat in that sweater."* Recognizing it as the critic, you think, *"Ah, my critic is sharing its opinion. Thank you for sharing, but I am going to wear what I want. I think I look fine."* The critic is appeased when you acknowledge it. Its message has been delivered and it backs off a little.

Every once in a while, the critic has a degree of truth so you can hear the message if you like, but ignore the commentary. Think of it as unwanted commentary by an old woman (or man) on the street. After a while, you can even predict what it's going to say. Same old, same old. When you get to this degree of separation, the commentary may even seem boring. It is less mesmerizing then, and you are free to let it go.

The Inner Nurturer

Just as each of us has an inner critic, we also have its opposite, a wise and nurturing voice. The inner nurturer is rooted in love, not fear. There is a distinct difference in the quality of its messages.

The only lasting solution to a harsh inner critic is to be connected to the wise nurturer inside, to listen to that voice over any other. Just like the cartoon with a devil on one shoulder and an angel on the other, you get to decide which voice you will listen to. Both have their convincing arguments, but only one offers genuine peace, and that is the voice of your wise inner self—the part that knows. We must listen deeply for this still small voice amidst the clamor of a loud and boisterous ego whose spokesperson is the inner critic.

On the next page are some characteristics of the wise, nurturing voice.

- It is always affirming.

- It will never lie or mislead you.

- It is never fearful.

- It is felt more than heard—a gut feeling or "knowing."

- It speaks unconditional love.

- It inspires patience.

- Silence may be the answer.

- You may feel as though your insides smile.

- It is connected to Source and contains all wisdom.

So test those voices inside you. Are they harsh and critical? Or patient and loving? Are the words affirming? Or degrading? Just as your inner critic uses the harmful voice of an authority figure, your inner nurturer will use the voice of supportive friends, relatives, or other influences.

If you have difficulty accessing your inner nurturer, there is an exercise following that may help. You might also want to spend time with people who are in touch with their own inner wisdom and notice how they access it, how they treat themselves, and the way you feel when you are with them. If you often nurture others, you may not be good at nurturing yourself or know how to access *your* inner nurturer. You might try nurturing yourself in the same ways that you love others and that you wish others would love you.

> ## As your focus shifts from critic to nurturer, you will find that you no longer need the same level of affirmation from outside; your inner nurturer will be providing it from within.

You can also access your inner nurturer through being present, through prayer and meditation, by practicing gratitude, and by focusing your attention on the above-the-line emotions. However you do it, remember that this, too, is a practice. You will get better at it over time.

Finding the Wise, Inner Nurturer

This is a meditation and visualization exercise. You will want to have some quiet time in a quiet place so you can give it all your attention.

Sit comfortably in a quiet space. Loosen any tight clothing. Close your eyes and begin to focus on your breathing. Take deep, full breaths. Scan your body, pay attention to any tense or sore spots. If you like, massage those areas a little, encouraging them to release. With your fingertips, massage your head, your forehead, your jaw muscles. Open your mouth wide, stretch your jaw, and let it find its natural resting place. Raise your shoulders up to your ears. Move them to the back and down making a circle. Do this several times. Let it all go and relax your whole body.

Now turn your attention to the center of your body. Intuitively feel into the place of your inner knowing.

Maybe it is in the center of your body. Maybe it is around your heart, at the base of your sternum, in your abdomen, or between your eyes. Remember that intuition is quiet, still, light, knowing. It is not loud or neon. What you sense will be just right. Imagine that this is the residence of your inner nurturer.

From that place of softness, imagine approaching a wounded being, a bird with a broken wing, a baby left crying and alone, an abandoned or injured animal. Show your care without using words. Notice what you do *in your body* to convey loving attention, to console, to soothe this precious being. This is your inner nurturer—the part of you that knows how to care for others and that can also care for you. Feel its presence. Allow yourself to be soothed by it. Know that you can access it at any time.

Reframing the Messages

So now you have an alternative to your loud and intense inner critic. You can the simply change your focus and listen for your inner nurturer's point of view. What does your inner nurturer tell you about:

- How you look
- Your ability to get beyond your breakup or divorce
- How you act toward your former partner
- Your sexuality
- Your desirability as a future romantic partner

* Your health/physical prowess/athletic ability

* How you take care of yourself

* Divorcing at the age you are

* Your ability to find work or create income

* Your ability to make and keep friends

If you don't know, describe things a wise and nurturing friend would tell you. *That* is the inner nurturer speaking using a friend's voice. Here is an example.

Critic: "You're just a divorced loser. Nobody wants to be around you."

Nurturer: "There are so many beautiful things about you. You have such tenacity and I am so proud of you. Many are drawn to your courageous heart."

Fortunately for us, the nurturer can carry on and on. Let it! The critic tends to drone in short quips and comments. Those you can ignore. Next time you hear your critic's voice, quickly ask, "What would my inner nurturer say to me?"

You can also counteract the critic's messages with affirmations as you did in the last chapter. You will learn more ways to refute the critic in the chapter on self-worth.

If you've had a particularly harsh critic, you may have developed a default emotional response like anger or fear or anxiety, whatever would be the natural result of the messages it has given you. Those emotions, and resulting behaviors like isolating or lashing out, can be more disheartening than the critical voice itself. The critic is only one small aspect of you. Let your wise self choose the voice you will listen to. Let a negative emotion remind you to choose a thought or affirmation that is more positive, which will call you to become present to your true nature. The critic may have its say, but it doesn't get to vote on your value.

Where Are You Now?

Critic or Nurturer—Who Wins?

I have a
debilitating critic.

I only listen to my
wise, inner nurturer.

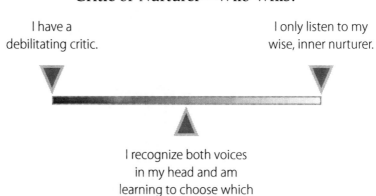

I recognize both voices
in my head and am
learning to choose which
I want to listen to.

Part Five

LEARNING FROM WHAT WENT WRONG

19

Marriage Is for Adults

Love asks independence of both parties — freedom,
not control, not guilt, not coercion, not manipulation.
Dependency is not love; it is dependency — it is an
abrogation of the essential responsibility of each
of us to grow up — to assume full responsibility
for our lives. Not to take on this challenge is a
flight from adulthood, no matter how mature a
person may be in other areas of endeavor.

— JAMES HOLLIS, *WHY GOOD PEOPLE DO BAD THINGS*

D id your partner act like a child in your relationship?
Did s/he lash out angrily when challenged, forget to
help with chores, let you do all the work, hide behind TV
or video games or the computer? Did you?

Many of the things that go wrong in a marriage can be
traced to a very common problem: One or both partners
are still looking for a love that they needed but did not
receive when they were growing up. Their love tank is running on empty.

We need love. Love is the fuel for life. Ideally, our early
years with mom and dad fill up our love tank so that when

we head out into the world, we go with a sense of fullness, knowing no other reality than being fully loved. But, of course, that ideal isn't always the reality. Dr. Elaine Aron, in her book *The Highly Sensitive Person*, estimates that just under half of all children have an insecure parental attachment,[14] meaning that without a fair amount of personal work, nearly half of us come to adulthood, and marriage, with a love deficit.

It is so common to arrive at marriage with an empty love tank that it doesn't seem all that unusual. Consider nearly every sitcom or love song. Often, without even realizing it, we find ourselves on a continual hunt to extract the love we need from our partner, who may in fact also be running on empty. Instead of coming to marriage with love to give, we come to get. That is a recipe for disaster.

A certain level of maturity is needed for marriage to go well. Just because our bodies look grown up doesn't mean our emotions, our thinking, our reactions, i.e. our ability to relate, have grown up with us. At age 43 we may have the love needs and relational skills of an 11-year-old. This doesn't bode well when mature responses are needed. We may arrive at marriage with more needs to be met than ability to meet the needs of another person. Learning about the ways you and your former mate fell short in the relationship will help you better understand what went wrong. This is the third turning point.

Since relationships always strive to balance themselves, it makes sense that if one partner is actively in a child role, the other will gravitate toward parenting behaviors. This is where most relationship problems start. We will take a look at both roles below. In what follows, see if you can identify your role and the role of your former partner.

The Child Role

When we are in the child role we absorb others' rules and expectations, perhaps complying out of a sense of duty or trying to live up to what we believe others expect of us within marriage. If you have not claimed yourself as the prime mover in your life, you have been bound by the expectations of others, including parents, family, pastors or church officials, schoolteachers, co-workers and bosses, or anyone you have taken as an authority, including your partner.

Below are two lists. One describes your being child-like in the relationship, the other describes what you may have felt if you were treated like a child by a parent-partner. See which is most like you.

I Acted Like a Child with My Former Spouse

- I didn't have my own opinions but conformed to what my partner wanted or thought.
- I tried to do what was expected so my partner wouldn't be disappointed or angry with me.
- I felt okay about myself if my partner was happy with me. I felt awful if s/he was upset with me.

- I was afraid to set limits with my Ex. If I did set limits, I was harsh and reactive with them.

- I didn't ask for what I wanted or needed. I just lived with the way things were.

- I didn't know how to deal with conflict. I would run away or stay silent.

- I let my Ex make any major decisions. I figured s/he knew more than I did.

- I often felt insecure, sometimes clingy.

- It was so much easier to let my partner take care of me, emotionally and/or financially, that I just let them.

- I was afraid of or felt ill-equipped to handle most responsibilities and was glad to let my partner take care of those things.

Although we are most often treated like a child because we act that way, there are times when, despite our best adult efforts, we are still treated like a child when in a relationship with a controlling person.

I Was Treated Like a Child by My Former Spouse

- My partner did not trust my judgment with the simplest things like money, parenting, or how I spent my time.

- I felt controlled or criticized.

- I wasn't consulted or trusted with decisions.

- If I made decisions on my own, my partner was angry, resentful, or withdrew.

- My partner was often critical and disapproving of me.

- I felt I couldn't do things right or good enough.

- My partner expected things to be done his or her way.

- My partner judged or resisted when I tried to better myself.

The child partner is often covert and passive, internalizing what the aggressive partner dishes out, allowing great harm to him or herself. This may lead to passive-aggressive behaviors.

This child role can express any or all of the following:

- Self-worth comes from making people happy
- Often deflect the nurturing they need
- Give more than they have to give, to their own detriment
- Martyr behavior

The Parent Role

The other side of this dynamic is the parent role. Do you see yourself in any of these statements?

I Acted Like a Parent with My Former Spouse

- I knew what was best for us so I just did it.

- I expected things to be done my way. I'd thought it through and my way was best.

- I tried to take care of most everything because my partner didn't participate.
- I expected an accounting for any money s/he spent.
- I wanted her/him to ask permission before spending money, going out with friends, or making a decision.
- I expected the house to be clean, the kids to be taken care of, meals prepared, and things done on time. I let him/her know if s/he didn't meet my expectations.
- There were some topics I refused to discuss.
- In conflicts I tried to overpower and win.

I Was Treated Like a Parent by my Former Spouse

- My partner wanted me to tell him/her what to do.
- I felt used and taken advantage of because my partner left me to handle everything.
- My partner blamed me if s/he wasn't happy.
- I sometimes felt my partner was invisible. I never really knew what s/he felt or thought.
- My Ex was often afraid that I would leave her/him.
- My Ex only thought of me as a paycheck.

Could you relate to any of these? I know there are some overlaps. You may have felt like the child in one area such as finances, but the adult in another like parenting. The bigger question is: How did you feel in the relationship most of the time?

The parent partner is more overt and aggressive, externalizing his or her behavior, sometimes by trying to control or dominate the other, and often all the more furious because the passive partner shrinks away or disappears.

This parental partner can show any or all of the following:

- Self-worth comes from being right
- Critical/perfectionistic
- Controlling/domineering
- High expectations/morally superior
- Lives by the rules, is justice oriented
- Self-righteous/condemning

The Parent Role and the Child Role Together

The parent–child dynamic creates an interesting, albeit dysfunctional, dance. It takes both parties to make this dance work. If one partner were to change and participate in a more mature way, the dysfunctional dance would fall apart.

It is commonly thought that the parent role is mature and the child role is immature, but that isn't so. Both partners of this imbalance are engaged in immature behaviors such as nagging, blaming, tattling, control, superiority, and dismissing, creating a vicious cycle that the two are helpless to get out of without help from the outside. New light from outside the system needs to be projected brightly into it to shine on the stuck places. Grounded in a solid sense of self, an adult doesn't feel the need to blame, judge, nag, or avoid, but is able to stand face to face and work out solutions. Until we learn more mature behaviors, we will do some form of either running (like a child) or conquering (like a domineering parent).

Under- and Over-Responsible

The overarching way that this dynamic plays out is in under- and over-responsible behaviors. The imbalance isn't always due to immaturity or dysfunction; sometimes one partner just has a bigger and more forceful personality that seems overpowering to a meeker partner. But the result is often the same. One takes charge; one backs away. Did you take on more responsibility, as your partner took less? Did you quit doing things because your partner didn't appreciate your efforts, tried to control the way you contributed, or raised the standard just as you got close to fulfilling his or her expectations? These are common complaints.

When there is an imbalance of responsibility in the relationship, it creates an imbalance of power that is hard to recover from. When an under-responsible partner lets important things slip, like filing the tax return or paying rent, the other partner naturally has to pick up the slack so things don't fall apart. If the under-responsible partner continues to check out of the relationship, forcing the more responsible partner to take charge, the gap continues to widen until it eventually breaks the relationship. The responsible partner grows tired of being so responsible, wants to have some fun, and perceives the child partner as a ball and chain holding them back. It works the other way, too. When the passive partner can no longer tolerate being controlled and criticized, s/he rebels against his/her controlling partner in an attempt to gain freedom. Often the passive person is only aware of the control of their partner and not their own passivity, which also contributed to the problem.

Identifying Over-Responsible Parent and Under-Responsible Child Patterns

On the following pages are two charts that will help you identify immature relational patterns that may have been present in your ended relationship. In the spaces provided, graph the behaviors you experienced by putting an **X** in the appropriate column. Most people lean toward one or the other of these behavior types, but you may find yourself doing some of each.

The Parent Role and the Child Role Together

CHILD BEHAVIORS	A Little	More Than A Little	A Lot
I didn't express my opinions.			
I did what was expected of me, and more.			
I felt bad if my partner was unhappy, especially if s/he was unhappy with me.			
I rarely set limits and often reacted in drastic ways.			
I rarely asked for what I needed and made do with what I got.			
I hated conflict. I would just stay quiet or walk away.			
I let my Ex make the decisions.			
I often felt insecure and needy in my marriage.			
I was afraid of adult responsibilities and was glad to defer those.			
I let my partner take care of me financially, emotionally, or otherwise.			

The Parent Role and the Child Role Together

PARENT BEHAVIORS	A Little	More Than A Little	A Lot
I expected things to be done my way. I'd thought it through and my way was best.			
I knew what was best for us, so I just did it.			
I tried to take care of most everything because my partner didn't participate.			
I expected the house to be clean, the kids taken care of, meals prepared, and for it to be done on time. I let him/her know if s/he didn't meet my expectations.			
I expected an accounting for any money s/he spent.			
I wanted her/him to ask me before spending money.			
There were some topics I refused to discuss.			
In conflicts I would try to overpower and win at all costs.			

Some Questions for You to Consider

- What do you notice after looking at your relationship in this way?

- On which side of this dynamic (parent or child) were most of your behaviors? How did that affect the way you showed up in your relationship?

- On which side of this dynamic was your partner? How was it to be partnered with that dynamic?

- In which areas did you balance each other out?

- How do you think you developed your way of relating?

- If you could change one thing about the way you participated in this dance, what would it be?

20

Leaving to Find Yourself

It takes courage to push yourself to places
that you have never been before,
to test your limits, to break through barriers.
And the day came when the risk it took to
remain tight inside the bud was more painful
than the risk it took to blossom.

— ANAÏS NIN

Did you feel confined by your marriage? Perhaps you ignored the problems, white-knuckled it, pretended things were good when they weren't, or looked the other way until you just couldn't do it any more. You didn't know what else to do, so you did what you'd always done until it was oh so clear that it wasn't going to work one more time. The relationship dynamics became a jail cell—your jail cell. Without different relating skills, you didn't know how to navigate your way to a more functional relationship. The costs were too high. The pain too great to stay.

Sometimes this confinement is felt most by the child partner who then becomes compelled to step into life in a more fulfilling way. As one participant in divorce class put it, "I parented my wife so well she eventually grew up and left home." For many people, once the drive to bust out of old unworkable dynamics awakens, it will not be quieted.

Sometimes this confinement is felt most by the parent partner or a caretaking partner who has grown weary of taking care of everything. If this is you, you likely want to let go of some of the responsibility and have a little fun— to experience more of life before it's over. To friends and family it may look like a mid-life crisis.

Either one may grow weary of the way things have been and in utter frustration say things like, "I can't be myself in this relationship. If it wasn't for you I would be happy. You've controlled me long enough. I don't even know who I am anymore. I have to go find myself. I'm sorry if I'm hurting you but it's time I quit taking care of everybody else and take care of me for a change." Sometimes those things are shared in a matter of fact adult manner. There are truly mature relationships that do end. But more often, there is a struggle to grow up and an internal fight for freedom taking place that manifests in lashing out, blaming, fighting, and those things are spoken from utter unhappiness.

Remember that both sides of this parent–child dance are relating with immature behaviors. Neither the child partner nor the parent partner have claimed themselves as the authority over their lives. Either one can have a strong drive to "leave home" and discover themselves, taking their partner, and perhaps friends and family, by complete surprise.

I Am the Seeker/Rebel

If you married young, or were in a particularly enmeshed or confining relationship, your need for separate space may be particularly strong. It's as if there is a part, or parts, of you that are demanding to be known and they need some white space around them to figure things out. This can lead to either an interesting adventure of learning about yourself, or be a terrifying leap into the unknown, and sometimes both. To you it is seeking, to others it is rebellious or just plain crazy. I will refer to both perspectives.

Here are some common feelings and behaviors for someone in this seeking/rebellious stage.

- ✓ Growing discontent
- ✓ Wanting to be on your own, out and away from the house, and away from your partner
- ✓ Feeling suffocated, especially when around your partner
- ✓ Thoughtful/preoccupied as you dream of a new future and maybe a new partner
- ✓ Focused on new friends and a new social life
- ✓ On the phone, online, or texting a lot
- ✓ Blaming your partner. "If it wasn't for you . . ."
- ✓ Demanding to run your own life. "I'll do it myself."
- ✓ Finding your personal style in fashion, music, friends, creative expression, etc.

✓ Avoiding daily responsibilities

✓ Foolish spending—maybe on a flashy car, roller blades, new wardrobe

✓ Strong desire to learn and try new things.

The metaphor of breaking out of jail fits the experience of breaking free in a marriage that has grown too tight. Remember that you *have allowed* these confines to be strengthened over time. You've put a number of the bars in place yourself. Construction starts when we are children. We come to the world through the veil of our parents' beliefs and culture. We take on their values, politics, religion, health practices, ideas about money, and many other things. We become immersed in them like a fish in water, not questioning how they apply to our own lives until much later. Wanting to please our parents, we conform to their wishes. At first this builds a safe structure inside us. It is a way of making the world predictable.

As the teen years approach we begin to revaluate the rules and values we've taken on from parents and other authority figures. *Do I really believe this? Or did I just adopt it because Ma, Pa, Pastor, Coach, Teacher, said I should?* We begin the process of choosing the rules and values we will take from childhood into adulthood, leaving behind the ones we do not want . . . often forcefully. This can seem very rebellious to those looking on from the outside because the trying-to-be-an-adult is rejecting some, if not all, of the things the parent, and sometimes the larger society, holds dear.

If we didn't complete this phase of picking and choosing our values for adulthood before marriage, there is a good chance we will complete it while in the marriage. A teen pushes against the restrictions of the parent, but in marriage the child-partner pushes against the real or imagined control of the parent figure. If you are the one being pushed against, it is important for you to realize that your partner is really pushing against internal limits that bind them, not you. You're just an easy target to blame.

I Was in Relationship with a Rebel/Seeker

Has your partner changed so much that you don't recognize him or her anymore? Has he changed the way he dresses, spends money, or spends his time? Does she want to leave the marriage to pursue romance with someone younger? Does he or she hate you and blame you for all their woes? These are typical behaviors of someone going through this stage.

It may be difficult to impossible to stay in close relationship with a rebelling partner. Caught in the upheaval of it all, he blames you as the cause of his inner turmoil, and doesn't hesitate to tell you so. You probably feel lost trying to figure out what to do, what to say, how to act, how to reach him. This is a very painful position to be in. You've done nothing out of the ordinary to cause this behavior and yet the person you love is lashing out and making you a villain. Everything was fine yesterday, or last week, and today they're moving out.

It may help to realize she is going through a necessary and normal stage of life. Unfortunately, there are no promises as to how things will play out once the phase completes. If you're waiting for a "seeking" partner to come to her senses, you could wait years. There is a more mature version of your partner on the other side of this rebellious phase, and if you have the patience and a lot of support, you might be able to wait it out. But it takes far longer than we imagine and most of us lose patience waiting.

As hard as it is to consider, the best thing for you to do is to focus on creating a happy life for yourself. Chances are you've needed a more independent life from your partner anyway and this is a wake-up call. This takes the pressure off your partner to change or make promises, and ultimately makes you more attractive—to yourself and others. If your partner decides to come back, s/he can join you in that happy life. If not, you've got a good start on a creating a life that is truly fulfilling.

With diligent effort to interrupt the unworkable parent–child dynamics by both partners, the relational dynamic can change, although it is rare. If you'd like to evaluate your relationship for possible reconciliation, please refer to my e-Book titled *Should We Reconcile?* at www.beyond divorce.com.

Conscious Breakthrough

I've referred to this period as the "seeking stage" because it starts with a deep desire to know yourself. I've referred to this period as a rebel stage because a lot of real and perceived rebellion takes place while you're in it. Now I will refer to it as a "breakthrough stage," as that is its ultimate goal. You are breaking out of the confines of your inner jail cell to the more spacious place where there is freedom of choice, freedom to make mistakes and learn from them, freedom to claim your right to yourself. You can't do that without busting out of the confines of childhood, any more than a butterfly can take wing without busting out of its cocoon. Part of the busting out entails choosing your beliefs anew, carefully determining the usefulness of each one to the next stage of your life.

Even though this is a required life stage, there are better ways than others to go through it. As with most things, we can be deliberate and conscious about it, realizing that we are going through a growth stage that will ultimately bring us to a new version of ourselves, or we can be unconscious and reactive, blaming others for our circumstances and inherent unhappiness. When we go through this phase, we may be consumed with our own experience, but we can still be aware of our behaviors and reactions.

It is important to remember that this experience is in you, and for you, and not about anyone else.

When we take responsibility for the decisions we've made, including those that have us feeling so disheartened, we can then make the changes necessary to have the life we want independent of anyone else's influence. This is the conscious way.

Blaming others for our unhappiness, or for being in the position we are, is the unconscious way. Personal responsibility marks the difference.

If you've allowed yourself to be controlled by a domineering person, you may feel anywhere from discouraged to enraged upon realizing how much personal power you've given away through the years. Conscious rebels take responsibility for changing things instead of blaming the other for their unhappiness and fleeing. It's hard to realize that we've gone along with our own imprisonment, but it's so empowering when we break free and begin to show up in life in a new way. It is empowering to take that power back.

Defending the Seeker/Rebel

In defense of the rebelling partner, it needs to be noted that adults do not *decide* to go through this stage any more than a teen decides to go through puberty. It just happens. It is our destiny to become our unique adult selves in order to take our specially reserved place in the world. To those looking on, the rebelling behavior seems irrational. *"If she would just calm down, give up this nonsense, and come back home, all would be fine."* The onlookers do not realize that her experience is being driven by something inside her that will not be silenced. If your relationship ended because of a perceived midlife crisis with its erratic behaviors, knowing this may help you understand why. If both of you only knew that on the other side of these behaviors was a mature loving adult, it would be easier to tolerate such a transition. We are uninformed and unprepared for this life-changing experience that ends so many marriages.

A Special Friend

The self-defining person may pursue a special friendship with someone he believes understands him in a way his partner never did. He feels deeply understood by this new friend. If the friend is of the opposite sex (which is not uncommon), to the casual observer it may seem like an affair. Often it doesn't start out that way, and with awareness and some safeguards it doesn't have to end up that way. This relationship can be an important ferry from childhood to adulthood.

Even though the intense feelings can cause the self-defining person to feel like he has found his long-lost soul-mate and want to run off and create a new life with this new friend, he might want to remember that these relationships have a very specific and time-limited purpose. This friend is there to witness, call forth, challenge, and support your development, filling the important role of listener, confidant, and friend. You are moving from the house of childhood to the home of adulthood, and this person is there to help you carry the boxes and decide where to put things. Then they will be gone, or fade far into the background. I hope you will enjoy this platonic relationship for what it is and not tie yourself physically (sex) or soulfully (commitments) in this temporary relationship.

Identify the Rebellious/Seeking Behaviors in Your Relationship

REBELLIOUS BEHAVIORS	A Little	More Than A Little	A Lot
Your level of rebellion			
Your level of ownership			
Your Ex's level of rebellion			
Your Ex's level of ownership			

Some Questions for You to Consider

* Was I in a rebellion stage when our relationship began and/or ended?
* Was my former partner in a rebellion stage when our relationship began or ended?
* How long did I feel discontent before I took action?
* Did I realize I was pushing against my own inner jail cell?
* Did I blame my partner for my unhappiness?
* What steps am I taking to find myself?

21

Three Trouble Spots

We are products of our past, but we
don't have to be prisoners of it.

— RICK WARREN, *PURPOSE DRIVEN LIFE:*
WHAT ON EARTH AM I HERE FOR?

There are, of course, many things that cause problems in a marriage. Some are carryover behaviors from the way we were raised. In our attempts to get the love, attention, nurturing, and praise we needed, we came up with brilliant strategies. Perhaps yours was trying harder— being the best at everything was how you earned approval. If so, you are likely still critical of yourself, and perhaps others also. Maybe you learned to spot needs and take care of others in order to get their love. If your parent was pre-occupied due to illness, work, or other life stresses, you may have done things like cleaned the house, taken care of your siblings, or cooked dinner for your parents to get some attention.

Even though these are brilliant strategies for a child, they cause trouble when brought into adult relationships. Below I've identified three of the most common behaviors learned in childhood that cause problems in marriage.

They are written from the point of view of relating to a partner with this behavior. You will want to turn it around if you were the one with the behavior. For example, if you identify yourself as a critical perfectionist, turn the section titled "If Your Partner Was a Critical Perfectionist" around to "I Was a Critical Perfectionist." This will help you understand the impact your behavior had on the relationship. At the end of the chapter you will have a chance to diagram the behaviors of both you and your former partner that were present in your ended relationship, so keep that in mind as you read.

If Your Partner Was a Critical Perfectionist

Was your partner critical about how you handled money, dressed, disciplined the kids, entertained, put the groceries away, kept the house, or did the laundry? If your partner was a perfectionist, you probably disappointed them regularly. Perfectionists have high standards for themselves and others, and can be harsh critics of those who don't live up to those standards. Perhaps your partner took charge of everything so s/he could be in control. Perhaps s/he gave the orders, expecting you to fulfill them, and let you know you were a disappointment when you failed.

Being in relationship with a critical perfectionist is exhausting. When one partner is a perfectionist, requiring things to be just so, with no allowances for doing things differently, the person on the other end has three basic options.

1. Give Up

Being a constant disappointment shreds your self-esteem. In response, you may have given up trying to meet your partner's expectations and perhaps checked out of the relationship emotionally, physically, or both, turning a deaf ear to the complaints. Or you may have remained physically present but with a part of your soul out the door.

2. Fight Back

If you had a little thicker skin, or didn't have a long history of living with that kind of criticism, you may have fought back. *"If you don't like the way I do it, do it yourself."* If your partner was also strong-headed, you may have had a test of wills, ending in emotional or physical abuse. Perhaps you tried to defend yourself early on and then gave up.

3. Get Sneaky

Perhaps the most common response to living with a controlling person is feigning compliance and doing what you want. Instead of telling your partner straight out that you wanted to buy new clothes with the tax refund, you just bought what you wanted and tried to cover your tracks. Although we resort to this type of behavior when we don't know another way, it is manipulative and irresponsible, and it undermines trust.

It is hard to be in a relationship with an irresponsible or manipulative partner. It's a little like trying to grab a bar of soap in the shower. They are hard to get a handle on, are great at twisting the truth, and are masters at covering up. When confronted, they often respond defensively by making the fault yours, not theirs.

The Positive Side of Perfectionism

There is a positive side of perfectionism, which is diligence and conscientiousness. Perfectionists take charge. They are great organizers. They have a critical eye and see the things that need improvement. Perfectionists have high ideals and high expectations and do their best to live up to them.

If Your Partner Was Absent

Other interesting dynamics come about with an absent partner. A person can be around every day but still be emotionally absent because they are consumed with their own interests or worries or just don't know how to make an emotional connection. If your partner didn't learn important relational skills or how to engage with others, you may have felt very alone in your marriage. Each of the absent behaviors on the next page could leave you feeling a different form of abandonment. Some of these are learned behaviors from the way we were raised.

Independence

If you (or your former partner) were thwarted in your attempts to get what you needed from your parents, you probably learned to be very independent and to take care of yourself. You may yet expect little from others and expect others to want little from you. Adult relationships require interdependence, which is the ability to give and take, and this is often hard for someone who is used to taking care of themselves.

Avoiding Emotions

Similarly, your former partner may have been preoccupied, distant or aloof, depressed, had an "all-business" style, or retreated intellectually into the familiar world of the mind rather than deal with messy emotional connections. S/he may have ignored or been unaware of your emotional needs because s/he was so out of touch with his or her own.

Physically Absent

Many jobs require a demanding travel schedule, odd shifts, and/or long hours away from home. Military service can also take a partner physically away from home. This puts unique stresses on a relationship and family when the absent partner returns and the system must adjust.

If Your Partner Was a Caretaker

Was your partner good at reading people? Did she seem to know what you wanted and give it to you without your even asking? This is the classic definition of a codependent—giving love in order to get love. Fearing rejection, a caretaking partner can be clingy and needy or try harder to please. A caretaker believes his actions are benevolent because he is doing such nice things, but caretaking is really a disguised controlling behavior. It is designed to put him in a position of being indispensable.

Unappreciated

If your former partner was a caretaker, she probably felt terribly underappreciated. When her care did not get her the love she wanted, she ran on empty a lot of the time. You likely either tried to show her how much you appreciated her efforts and when you couldn't fill her up you stopped, or you got so used to her doing things for you that after a while you didn't even notice her efforts. Caretakers often sacrifice more than they have to give, even to the point of being a martyr, at great loss to themselves.

Becoming Selfish

A common reaction to the codependent person is to become more selfish and indulgent. When we don't have to show up and participate in a relationship, we often don't. If your partner did things before you even asked for them, you may have given up trying to do things for yourself and expected they would be done for you. On the other hand, your caretaking partner may not have allowed you to participate, but then blamed you for not carrying your share of the load.

The Positive Side of Caretaking

The positive side of caretaking is a genuine love and care for others. Nurturers are often tuned in to the needs of others in the ways most people are not. We need nurturers in our world.

Identify the Behaviors in Your Relationship

On the graph below, mark the behaviors that were present in your ended relationship. Remember that this doesn't have to be exact. You are merely creating a snapshot.

TWO SIDES OF THE DANCE	A Little	More Than A Little	A Lot
My partner was a critical perfectionist			
I was a critical perfectionist			
My partner was an absent partner			
I was an absent partner			
My partner was a caretaker			
I was a caretaker			

Some questions for you to consider.

- Did you try to live up to your partner's expectations? What did it feel like when you couldn't?

- Did your partner want more from you? How did you respond?

- Did you want more from your partner? How did it feel when you didn't get it?

- Did you feel resentful and taken for granted?

- What will you do differently now that you know this?

How Are You Doing?

How adult do you feel in general, in your relationships?

I feel like a child,
or a parent, most
of the time.

I often feel like I
act and respond in
an adult manner.

I'm still working through old patterns,
but at least I'm aware of them now.

22

Broken Boundaries

Evaluating the benefits and drawbacks of any relationship is your responsibility. You do not have to passively accept what is brought to you. You can choose.

— DEBORAH DAY

Did you allow yourself to be hurt in your marriage because you did not understand the importance of having boundaries or know when and how to use them? Maybe you didn't know that not only *could* you set limits, but that you *should*.

> **Boundaries are necessary to protect all of who you are—your hopes, your dreams, your heart, and more.**

It is not only your right but your responsibility to limit anything that gets in the way of living out your hopes and dreams. This includes your Ex, your kids, your mother, and your schedule. In this chapter, you will learn different types of boundaries and when and how to use them.

First, see if you identify with any of these characteristics of people who can't or won't set boundaries.

- Feels like a victim
- People pleaser
- Gets taken advantage of; a doormat
- Life feels out of control
- Feels responsible for everyone; rescuer or caretaker
- Can't say no
- Takes on too many things; tired
- Feels invisible and without a clear identity

Did you recognize yourself in that list? If so, this chapter will be of particular interest.

What to Protect

Maybe you understand the need for boundaries but aren't sure what you should protect. Here are a few ideas:

Your heart. You know how you want to be treated and don't settle for less. You require respect from those around you. Your self-esteem is a vital commodity right now and must be protected.

Your time. Your precious time is in constant demand: a friend in need, a deadline that can't wait, endless appointments, the local charity that wants you to volunteer once again, even a child who wants you to get him a drink rather than get it himself. It's okay to be picky about how you spend your time. Asking others to pick up the slack is okay, too.

Your health. You need time to prepare good food, get some exercise, and rest, especially now. Your vital energy is your most precious commodity. Anything that saps your energy needs to be limited.

Your wealth. You need a certain amount of money with which to function. You may want to soothe yourself by buying new things or giving to others, in order to feel better. Anything that puts a strain on your finances should be limited.

Your dreams, goals, gifts, and talents. You are a unique individual with special gifts and talents to give. Who are you without your dreams? Protect them.

Friendships and family. You want to protect your children from drama, harmful conversations, overscheduling, and anything that would tax their hearts, time, health, gifts, and talents.

Now that you know some of the things you might protect, let's talk about how to do that.

Boundary Basics

There are many options for limiting the harmful stuff that comes your way. You can use words, physical distance, emotional distance, and time. Time adds urgency and a framework as you will see.

Boundaries come in varying degrees and intensity. You won't need to move to another country the first time you set a limit. A simple *No* may suffice. I suggest that you start with the simplest boundary, increasing the time and distance as needed.

Saying No. The first and most basic boundary is the word *no*. Every two-year-old knows it and will say it often just to test this new power. It is an empowering skill to have. *No* is a line in the sand. It lets others know how you expect to be treated and what you will and will not do.

You can learn a lot about someone when you tell them no. Do they hear you and honor your *no*, or are you shamed, manipulated, attacked, or overridden when setting your limits? Be prepared for an angry outburst the first time you say *no* to someone who hasn't heard that from you before. This may be another *feel the fear and do it anyway* moment for you.

In the same way, you can learn a lot about yourself when someone says no to you. How do you respond? Do you accept it? Or do you believe they owe you and don't have the right to say *no*? Do you manipulate, control, use guilt, or bully? Do you honor them by honoring their choice even if you really, really want them to do whatever it is you are asking of them? The mature response to *no* is to be sad rather than mad, to grieve it and let it go. *"I really wanted that. I'm terribly sad that I can't have it."*

You don't need to justify your reasons for saying *no*. You alone decide what does or does not contribute to your well-being. Can you say *no* to someone without feeling guilty? Can you say *no* as easily as you say *yes*? If not, there's more for you to learn. *No* is a powerful word. Use it and observe. You will learn a lot.

Saying *No* to Yourself. There will be times when you need to say *no* to yourself, to pressures emanating from within that would have you overextend yourself or partici-pate in harmful behaviors.

Layla clearly needed to say *no* to herself when she kept checking her husband's credit card purchases, cell phone bills, and his Match.com profile online (where she felt he greatly misrepresented himself). Every time she saw a charge for another dozen roses sent to his girlfriend or for the cruise they were scheduled to take—while she and the kids struggled to make ends meet—it set her back many steps in her recovery. If Layla could have said *no* to her own impulses and put all that energy into her own recovery, she would have been a lot happier. Her Ex was going to do what he was going to do regardless of whether she checked on him or not.

Emotional and Energetic Boundaries. Emotional boundaries are needed when you have to be in close contact with someone but still need to keep your distance. Some divorcing couples are forced to stay in their home together because of financial constraints. If you are a parent, the two of you will have ongoing interactions. In those instances, emotional boundaries are necessary for separation and pro-tection. An emotional boundary creates a buffer between your heart and the other. It can be maintained by things you do, such as not speaking, limiting eye contact, limiting communication, maintaining a business tone, or not sharing aspects of your life that you would have disclosed in the past, allowing yourself and your partner more privacy. Emotional boundaries may also be needed when in close proximity to each other outside the home, such as the sidelines of your child's sporting event, the mediator's office, or at the wedding of a mutual friend. Having these kinds of boundaries does not mean you are being petty. You are protecting your vulnerable self until, if and when, it is safe to relate more personally again.

Some people find it useful to erect an energetic barrier between themselves and the other person. One of my favorites is to imagine a circle of protection around me. Within the circle I am connected to All Good, safe and protected. Things that stress me remain outside the circle and don't enter unless I allow them. I can make the circle as large or as small as I like depending on the amount of protection I desire.

Physical and Time Boundaries. If you are with someone who cannot or will not honor the boundaries that you set verbally, you may have to take another step such as inserting physical distance between you. Adding time to the physical boundaries makes them more real. You know you are protected for a given length of time, and the other knows s/he has X length of time to make important changes.

Physical boundaries are things like going to another room, staying at a friend's house, renting an apartment, or going to a safe house. In troubling circumstances a restraining order may be necessary to enforce the boundary.

Physical boundaries are made more effective by adding time limits. Notice how these boundaries increase incrementally.

- Walk into a separate room for 30 minutes.
- Go to a motel for a night.
- Stay with a friend or relative for a month.
- Rent an apartment for a year.
- Buy a house in a different state for an undetermined length of time.
- Move to another country.

If you live separately and still need to set limits, your incremental boundaries may look like this:

- Do not call me during working hours.
- I will accept your texts but not emails or phone calls.
- You are not to contact me for a _____(week, month, year).
- My attorney will take all communications from you from now on.

Defining Your Boundaries

1. Inside the circle on the next page, or in your journal if you need more room, list all the things you are protecting. We have talked about several things throughout the chapter.

2. On the outside of the circle write things that do, or try to, break into your life, time, and heart and harm the very things you are trying to protect. Include things that others expect of you or that you expect of yourself: bullying behaviors, harsh comments, poor self-care, an extreme schedule, etc. I've provided two as examples.

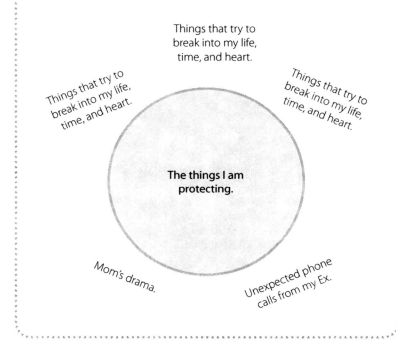

Things that try to break into my life, time, and heart.

Things that try to break into my life, time, and heart.

Things that try to break into my life, time, and heart.

The things I am protecting.

Mom's drama.

Unexpected phone calls from my Ex.

To know if an item goes inside or outside the circle, check in with your body. If you feel tightness in your chest or throat, if your heart beats faster, or if it simply doesn't feel good, that item belongs outside of the circle. After a time of seeing your boundaries on paper like this, you will intuitively feel when one of your boundaries is crossed, allowing you to respond proactively before any harm is done.

The ability to use boundaries with ease is an important and empowering life skill. Remember that you have goals, dreams, and talents to protect. Boundaries will help you preserve your vital energy (turning point four) for creating a life you love (turning point five).

Delayed Reaction

Sometimes we are numb to the pain that comes from being violated. We don't recognize it as a violation either because we are out of touch with our boundaries to begin with or because our boundaries have been regularly violated and that is just the way things are in our experience. Maybe you've just woken up to the reality that you have been used, taken for granted, or perhaps even abused for years. We react very slowly at times, just now understanding what happened thirty years ago. It takes time and maturity for us to become current with our emotions and connect them with previous offenses. It can be a shocking discovery to realize that we could have done something about much of what happened to us throughout our marriage, if we'd known to do so. It is hard, but still worthwhile to admit that we have been asleep and allowed many of these abuses to happen. Any time we can own our experience, we develop a little more freedom. As you get better with boundaries, your delay will shorten to months instead of years, with the goal of being able to speak up for yourself right there in the moment. There is little that is as empowering as standing in the middle of your "yard" feeling confident, safe, and in control of your world.

When we use boundaries well, we keep the good close for our use, and the bad out and away from us. Some of the good we need to let in is love and care from others, positive information that helps us learn and grow, and good self-care. We don't want to get mixed up by letting the bad in and keeping good things away. Things like the hurtful comments of others need to stay on the outside of your "yard." Every once in a while it is good to ask:

What good can I let in today?

What is the bad I need to keep out today?

How Are You Doing?

How are you at using boundaries?

I either have no boundaries or I feel mean when I set limits.

I set boundaries well. I can say *no* as easily as I say *yes*.

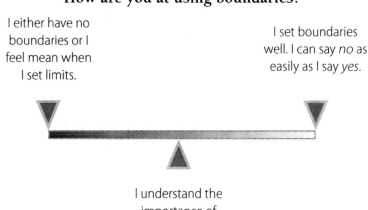

I understand the importance of boundaries and I'm getting much better at setting limits.

23

Toward Mature Relating

A relationship should serve the growth of each party
toward becoming more nearly who he or she is capable of
becoming. I do not see that relationship in which people
"take care of each other" as worthy of the name of
relationship, at least not a loving, mature relationship.

— JAMES HOLLIS, *WHY GOOD PEOPLE DO BAD THINGS*

We've looked at several ways your participating in a parent–child dynamic may have affected your relationship. You saw how being absent either physically or emotionally limited your ability to connect. Your relationship may have limped along for years under the weight of these unwieldy behaviors, until it finally broke. Most of us don't realize the impact of our dysfunctional ways of relating until something breaks.

When we get away from expecting relationships to heal childhood wounds and deficits, and instead turn toward their larger purpose of both companionship and personal growth, relationships become far more meaningful. They serve us rather than drain us.

Mature relating is where all of our discussions have been leading. This is the culmination of turning point four. Divorce revealed the holes in your heart that needed healing, some immaturities that needed growing up, and behaviors that needed to change. As you continue to do your personal work, you will one day enter life in a completely different way. Life will still be its usual challenge but you will interact with it on a different level and with a completely different set of tools in your belt. The problems you will face will be more meaningful. No longer at the mercy of child behaviors, you have the opportunity to create something good for yourself—turning point five.

Traits of a Mature Person

So what traits does a mature individual possess, and how do those traits express in relationship? A mature person:

- Relates to others as equals, being neither one-up nor one-down.
- Appropriately expresses a wide range of emotions.
- Takes responsibility for their attitudes and behaviors.
- Apologizes when they've done harm.
- Gives cheerfully from a non-controlling, non-needy, grounded sense of self.
- Easily asks for help and support.
- Says *yes* without coercion and *no* without guilt.

* Knows that the response to not getting
  what they want is to grieve it rather than to
  demand, control, manipulate, or pout.

* Doesn't allow themselves to be manipulated
  or controlled; understands the usefulness of
  boundaries in a relationship.

* Is able to self-soothe and doesn't expect
  their partner to be their all in all.

* Can forego immediate gratification for
  long-term rewards.

* Gives self and others room for weaknesses
  and to learn from mistakes.

* Initiates difficult conversations in order to
  solve problems.

* Has access to their inner wisdom and is
  able to ask, "What is appropriate now?"
  when situations change.

Inner wisdom is key. Being an adult means coming into full interactivity with the world and become completely and uniquely ourselves. When mature, we have the skills to choose a partner who is ready, willing, and able to support our goals, and we are able to support theirs.

Finding Our Way to the Adult Self

Growing up is not an overnight process. It takes time and continued effort. None of us really knows where to start. Fortunately life always brings us what we need. Growing up requires little more than the willingness to leap each hurdle as it comes. Were you a stay-at-home parent and now need to find a job? Who will you need to be to accomplish this feat? As you face this challenge you mature into the person who can meet it. Do you need to tell a controlling person that you will no longer tolerate certain behavior? Unearthing your assertiveness brings maturity in that area. One step at a time you behave your way to a more mature self. It can be tough work. If you grow weary, enlist your supportive people who will champion you when you want to give up.

Living from Our Adult Self

Those who do the work of becoming adults have freedom and opportunities that the less mature only dream of. Until then, we find ourselves bouncing back and forth between the "needs" of our inner child: "I need a hug. I need a job. I need this divorce to be done. I need more money. I need more time with my kids. I need my mother to leave me alone," and the "shoulds" of the parent voices: "I should be over her by now. I should be able to be around him without falling apart. I shouldn't worry so much about money. I shouldn't cry so much. I shouldn't eat that third piece of chocolate cake. I shouldn't go to the bar again tonight. I ought to clean my house." The list goes on and on. Do you recognize any of those? Those two voices are often so loud that the adult voice, your inner wisdom, gets drowned out entirely.

Leaving Old Habits

Remember that in order to have "different" you must do "different." It will take effort to implement a new way of doing things as old ways can be very ingrained, but I hope you won't give up. Be gentle with yourself as you learn. Below are some things you can do to break old habits.

If You Were a Critical Perfectionist

Since perfectionists must have everything just so, a behavior that will help bring balance is to leave things undone—like the dishes in the sink, your bed unmade, toys strewn about, or your pencils unsharpened. See if you can do this for an entire week. Notice your reaction as you do. Do you feel anxious? Nervous? Compelled to *do* something? Are you tense? Is your stomach tight? Perhaps your former spouse experienced something similar while in relationship with you. See if you can relax. Remember to breathe. Laugh at yourself and the absurdity of it all. Spend some time with your kids or friends. Write about what you learn in your journal.

If You Were an Absent Partner

If you were an absent partner you will want to make an effort to consciously connect to others. No doubt there are people in your life who would like to know you better. Challenge yourself by reaching out. Call a few friends and just talk. Ask them how they are doing. Listen for how they feel. Notice what happens inside you. Are you anxious? Does it seem stupid? Do you want to get off the phone? As much as you can, hang in there and notice your reactions. Notice how the person on the other end isn't all that focused on you, but is focused on his or her end of the conversation. Share something you don't think he or she wants to know about, just because you can. See how they respond. Write about your experience in your journal.

If You Were a Caretaker

Caretakers have a really hard time letting other people care for them. This is your opportunity to ask someone to do something just for you, maybe pick up your dog from the vet, give you a ride somewhere, or just come over and watch TV. Since you probably try to do everything anyone asks of you, you also want to practice saying *no*. Think of someone you need to set a limit with, and do it. Notice what happens for you. Does it seem selfish? Do you feel anxious? Are you worried that they won't like you? Do you want to jump right back in and take care of something or someone? The first step to changing a behavior is to become aware of it. Let your uncomfortable feelings alert you to the behavior that needs to change. This is a time for you to take your energy that you have spread all over everywhere, and bring it home to yourself. It's yours. Caretakers are out of balance when it comes to giving. If the changes you make feel selfish to you, it's probably just right.

If You Were in Breakthrough

Notice your predisposition toward blaming others when you feel uncomfortable. You may blame your Ex, your parents, the courts, or other authority figures. When you notice yourself blaming, turn your focus inward and ask, "What do I need to take responsibility for?" Notice the fears that arise. Notice the conflict you feel between wanting to retreat back to the comfort of your inner jail cell and the drive to leave it.

We participate in these behaviors—perfectionism, keeping to ourselves, caretaking, blaming—because they relieve the anxiety that builds up if we don't. If your anxiety gets too great, you may reach for your favorite form of comfort, whether it is alcohol and drugs, comfort foods, spending money, sex, or retreating back into the very behavior you're trying to get out of. Let your anxiety remind you of what you're trying to do. Try again. Behave your way to success. Mastering these balancing behaviors will bring you closer to your adult self, which is the ultimate goal of the third turning point.

The Ultimate Solution

Responding to life from our adult selves not only provides relief from the needs and the shoulds, it allows us to live without the drama of a life of reactivity, bouncing between one painful circumstance and another. If you want to find peace, you will want to seek the peace that is independent of your circumstances. Until we find that peace we are subject to the duality of life where good easily turns bad and happy easily turns sad. The present is your portal to the calm. It is your link to that which is unchanged and undiminished by circumstances. We find it by focusing on it. We find it in stillness.

Once you find that peace beneath your circumstances, life may continue to rush hurriedly and chaotically around you, but at your center you remain calm and virtually untouched. It is the space between the past and the future, where there is nothing to *do*; only your true self to *be*. It's worth the effort to find this place daily. There are many books on the subject and gurus who would guide you.

You've learned a lot in this section of the book. Did you recognize behaviors that you and your Ex participated in that may have contributed to the demise of your marriage? We've covered the various aspects of child behaviors, the troublesome rebel/seeking stage, and now, what it means to be an adult.

The chart on the next page[15] captures characteristics of all three stages. Please review them and then move to the exercise "Identifying Your Relational Stages."

Category	Child Stage	Seeking Stage	Maturity
Rules	I should.	I won't.	I choose.
View of Self	I'm not okay (unless you say I am).	I don't know if I'm okay, but you suck!	I'm okay. You're okay.
Approach to Life	I don't know.	I know it all.	I have new information. Now what do I choose?
Identity	Who am I?	I have to be who I am.	I understand and live out of who I am.
Abilities	Do it for me.	I'll do it myself!	Let's do it together.
Power	You have the power.	I'm seeking my power.	I understand my personal power and live it with grace and ease.
Relating	Don't leave me. Make me happy. I do what is expected so you'll love me.	Leave me alone. I'm unhappy and it's your fault! I don't care what you want.	We can be together and apart. I create my own happiness. I care about me and I care about you.

Identifying Your Relational Stages

After you review the characteristics above, graph these three behaviors as they showed up in your ended relationship. This is a compilation of the graphs you've completed in this section and adds to the level of mature relating that was in your relationship. It is most helpful to analyze the relationship as it was toward the end. This is usually when dysfunctional behaviors were most present.

GRAPHING YOUR BEHAVIORS	A Little	More Than A Little	A Lot
I participated as a child.			
My partner participated as a child.			
I was a rebel.			
My partner was a rebel.			
I acted as an adult.			
My partner acted like an adult.			

Here are some questions for you to consider

- How did your behavior impact the marriage?
- How did your former partner's behavior impact the marriage?
- Did the two of you have similar or opposing styles?
- If you have children, how might the styles of you and your former partner impact your children?
- What is one thing you can do to bring yourself more toward maturity?

Taking what you've learned about what went wrong—the third turning point, we move into the fourth turning point: self-discovery, and reclaiming your power.

Part Six

RECLAIMING YOUR POWER

24

Forgive to Let Go

*Not to forgive is to be imprisoned by the past,
by old grievances that do not permit life to proceed
with new business. Not to forgive is to yield oneself
to another's control . . . to be locked into . . . outrage
and revenge . . . escalating always. Forgiveness . . .
extracts the forgiver from someone else's nightmare.*

— LANCE MORROW, THE CHIEF: A MEMOIR
OF FATHERS AND SONS

Moving into forgiveness so soon after processing grief and anger may be difficult. That's understandable. These emotions are not easy, and moving through them is not merely an intellectual exercise. It is deep soul-shifting work that takes time. I suggest that you work through this chapter as best you can for now and revisit it again later, perhaps in a month or two, to see how far you've come.

Forgiving may be one of the most difficult parts of your journey. It is difficult in part because we don't understand the benefits. We often aren't sure just what it is, or what it's supposed to do. It just feels hard.

I've often suggested that you be gentle with yourself. That holds with your ability to forgive, also. You've probably been told that you *should* forgive, after all it's the *right* thing to do. But what if you can't? Perhaps you confuse forgiving with trusting. They are two different things and we will talk about the differences. In the end, you will forgive what you can for now. You will heal and grow and forgive some more. It may not happen all at once, and that's okay.

So what is forgiveness anyway?

Two Levels of Forgiveness

I believe that there are two levels of forgiveness. The first is on a human-to-human level—something that we *do* for ourselves and others. The second is Divine, or spiritual. It is something to which we release ourselves—a way of *be*-ing in the world. In this chapter we will talk about the human side of forgiveness. Until we are able to access our highest human virtues like tolerance, kindness, humility, and compassion, we don't have what we need to release into Divine Forgiveness anyway. We leave that for another discussion.

What's in It for Me?

Forgiveness has little to do with the person who is making you miserable. It's for *you*—your heart, your happiness, your ability to get on with your life. Forgiveness helps to restore positive thoughts, feelings, and behaviors, first toward yourself and later toward the person who hurt you. This is an integral part of letting go, a major component in the fourth turning point—reclaiming your power.

When you are able to access forgiveness, the internal churning stops. The constant internal arguments with your former partner are no longer necessary and fade away. All the energy you've put into keeping track of the other's moves and motives—and adjusting your life to dodge them, track them, or attack them—is over. Forgiveness spills over to positive behaviors, just as non-forgiveness spills over to negative behaviors. Forgiveness is good for you, good for others, and good for our world.

If you dwell on hurtful events and grudges, vengeance and hostility may take root. If you allow negative feelings to crowd out positive ones, you may find yourself swallowed up by your own bitterness or sense of injustice. Your mind remains clogged with the continuous replay of hurtful events. You can become so wrapped up in the wrong that you can't enjoy what's right. You may become depressed or anxious, or feel that your life lacks meaning or purpose. You may find yourself at odds with your spiritual beliefs. Perhaps most important, you may lose valuable and enriching connectedness with others. Your lack of forgiveness won't confine itself to just the person who hurt you but will infect other relationships as well. Harboring hatred, bitterness, or non-forgiveness is like taking poison and hoping the other person will die. It harms you far more than it harms the other.

To forgive is to release a debt. Your former partner did hurt you. He or she likely "owes you big time." S/he likely should pay. But instead of allowing your life and happiness to be held hostage until that payment comes, you can release the other—and at the same time, release your-self. You release the debt for your sake. Releasing the debt means you don't need the other person to tell you they're sorry, "take it back," repay the money, or anything else. You don't need to extract anything from your former partner in order to move on or be happy. Letting go of grudges, bitter-ness, and the desire for revenge makes way for compassion, kindness, and peace. Forgiveness is a gift you give yourself. When you forgive, you put yourself in the driver's seat of your own happiness.

Forgiveness can lead to:

- Less stress, lower blood pressure, less fatigue
- Healthier relationships
- Greater spiritual and psychological well-being
- Fewer symptoms of depression, anxiety, and chronic pain
- Less risk of alcohol and substance abuse, including prescription drugs
- Better sleep
- Freedom in all important areas

Forgiving Others

Forgiveness is not necessarily a feeling, although the peace-ful feelings do eventually come. *Forgiveness is a choice.* It is a decision to let go of resentment and thoughts of revenge.

It is a decision to let go of the hurt and turn toward creating new meaning. Forgiveness can lessen the grip your Ex has on you and help you focus on the positive parts of your life. If you wait until you feel like forgiving, you may remain stuck with these painful and limiting feelings for a very long time.

Forgiving may seem like letting your partner off the hook. But in reality it does not justify or minimize the wrong done to you. Instead it acknowledges it. Forgiveness says, *"You hurt me, and I forgive (release) you. I will take charge of fixing it."* It doesn't deny the hurt or pretend it didn't happen. It also doesn't deny the other person's responsibility. What it does is keep you from remaining hostage to them until they get around to fixing it.

By way of example, if someone borrows your car and wrecks it, you could sit around fuming, and without wheels, until that person feels like fixing it. Depending on their resources, this could take a fair amount of time, and that is if they are willing. Someone who is not willing can take forever. If you forgive the offender this debt, you accept that the car is broken, get it fixed, and get on with your life. Of course it's not fair. They should fix it, but they aren't going to. You can stay stuck and subject to their whims, or you can take charge and move on.

Forgiving does not mean that you must trust again, or reconcile. It doesn't mean you must "forgive and forget." I hope you do remember so you won't put yourself in a position to be hurt again. Too many people are hurt when they blindly trust again without considering the character of the person in whom they are trusting. Knowing who and when to trust is another important life skill to learn or relearn.

Expressing the Feelings

So what do you do with all those feelings? Being on the receiving end of an injustice is just not right. Betrayals hurt. Injustices bring rage. Being ignored or put down undermines your self-esteem. Before you can get to forgiveness you must claim your right to your feelings. You have a right to them. Fully take your own side, even if you know the ways you contributed. This will help you feel the full range of your feelings. There are many ways for you to express. If you wrote your anger or grief letters, and especially if you read them to a supportive person, you've done some of this. You can talk to friends and family, or your therapist. A divorce group is an ideal setting. Some people find it useful to write or talk to God about it, pouring out all the hurt, fury, and frustration. Write about your feelings and the injustices in your journal if that helps. Keep writing until you feel some relief.

Exercises for Forgiving Others

It's tough to forgive when we've been hurt deeply. There are so many conflicting emotions. We may know it's the right thing to do. We may believe we *should* but don't know how. The following exercises below will help.

Naming the Obstacles to Forgiveness

Sometimes we are afraid to forgive for reasons we are not even aware of. Working with these sentence stems can help flush out some of the reasons. Complete each sentence with the first thing that comes to mind.

- If I forgive (name), then_____.
- I don't want (name) to think_____.
- I don't want to forgive, because I don't want to let go of _____.
- If I forgive, I might feel _____.
- Not forgiving allows me to_____.

Although we may not like to think so, we're really not all that different from the people who have hurt us. We all make mistakes, are insensitive at times, and regress under stress by acting in immature ways that later embarrass us. If we're capable of causing similar harm, how can we hold a grudge against someone else?

I know it's hard to step into someone else's shoes, especially if you don't like them very much, but if you can identify why your former partner has done some of the things s/he has done it may help you be more empathetic and move closer to forgiveness.

Understanding Your Partner's Experience

Consider five events or beliefs that may have contributed to your Ex doing things that were hurtful or did not make sense. Examples: parent died, health problems, lost job, empty nest, moving, estranged family member, feeling abandoned. The two big fear producers during divorce are threatened finances and parenting time, so I will use those as examples.

Examples: Partner One realizes she is going to be on her own financially for the first time, fears she can't make ends meet, and is angry to be put in this position. Partner Two realizes how much of his children's lives he's missed by working so much to provide for them, so he fights for more parenting time and comes across as aggressive.

Select one factor and write, or talk to, someone about it.

Some Questions for You to Consider

- Does it help to see the contributing factors?

- What insights did you gain?

- How might your new understanding help you going forward?

Writing a Forgiveness Letter to Your Ex

In this exercise, write a Forgiveness Letter just as you did for grief and anger. Before you start, consider ahead of time which part of you will do the writing. Will it be your wise nurturer, your critic, your adult, a child part, or some other aspect? As best you can, let your writing come from a compassionate part of you. In your letter, tell your Ex that you have chosen to forgive him or her and why. Describe how you intend to view future incidents. You may want to include the things for which you want to offer forgiveness *and* things for which you would like forgiveness, which you identified in preparation for your grief and anger letters. Your Forgiveness Letter can offer more closure than either your grief or anger letters, as it sums up all three emotions.

It may be useful to actually send this letter (as opposed to the grief and anger letters, which you should not send), but each case is different. Use your own judgment. I don't recommend sending your first draft. You will want to wait until you feel deep and true forgiveness so you don't end up sending an anger letter in disguise, which will only serve to escalate things. Saying, *"I forgive you for being such an insensitive louse for the last twenty years"* is not going to help. You might ask the opinion of an objective third party to make sure what you've written is in the spirit of true forgiveness before sending it. When we're "in it," it's easy to fool ourselves. It might be useful to let it sit for a week or even a few months, and re-evaluate before deciding whether to send it. First and foremost, writing this letter is for you. Whether you send it or not is unimportant.

Forgiving Yourself

Often, the hardest person to forgive is yourself. You've probably said to someone, *"That's okay. I know you didn't*

mean it." The same frailty and shortcomings that you readily forgive in others, you may not forgive in yourself.

Failure to forgive yourself can result in:

- Continuing to be hurt by unresolved pain
- Behaving in ways that harm you
- Low self-esteem
- Being overly defensive or distant in
  relationships
- Unnecessary guilt and remorse that wear
  you down
- Self-destructive behavior
- Inability to forgive others

Remember that forgiveness is releasing a debt. That
applies to forgiving yourself, too. Those of us who keep
that whip handy believe that flogging is our payment plan.
But it's a useless plan.

Can you put the whip down? Let yourself off the hook?

Can you offer benevolent forgiveness to the person who
needs it the most (you!)? Remember Maya Angelou, if
you could have done better, you would have done better.
Period. You're only human.

The biggest obstacle to forgiving yourself is the belief
that you should be able to do things right all the time or
that you should somehow have answers you do not have.

Perfection is overrated. If you find yourself saying "should" a lot, question that. *"I should have known better. I should have done better. I shoulda, shoulda, shoulda."* Really? Given what you knew at the time you should have done better? Probably not. What you can do now is use your mistakes as fodder for growth in the future.

Forgiving yourself has many benefits:

✓ No longer beating yourself up for mistakes
✓ Releasing hurtful memories and painful events
✓ Developing an optimistic view of the future
✓ Realizing you have value and worth
✓ Loving yourself in healthy ways
✓ Loving others in new and different ways
✓ Developing respect for yourself

It can take a long time to forgive yourself, yet only when you forgive yourself can you truly forgive others. Consider that you may be having this experience that requires you to forgive yourself as a precept to healing some lost or forgotten part of yourself. Forgive yourself and lay claim to your wholeness.

Making a Self-Forgiveness List

When you first consider the idea of forgiving yourself, you may have a long list of things to work through. Most of us have a backlog of things we're ashamed of and have tried to hide away.

Some of the things for which you will want to forgive yourself could include the way you've behaved or spoken to your partner or children; acts of violence both large and small; putting up with bad behavior for too long; wasting irretrievable years that could have been used to start a career, save for retirement, or reclaim your health; ending the marriage; or not being able to keep the marriage together. Anything for which you feel guilty could be included.

I suggest making a list of all the things for which you want to forgive yourself, and add to it regularly. Having your list on paper gets it out of your head, and you can look at it more objectively. If you leave it in your head it takes on a gnawing, ambiguous, pervasive quality that is always there, never resolving. I know a woman who makes a list daily, and forgives herself each night before bed. "I forgive myself for . . ."

As you work through your storehouse, the emotional burden will lessen and events will become more current. That is, you will be working with things from today rather than from decades ago. Until that point, just work through the items as you think of them, whether they were from earlier in your life, your divorce, or the day you've just had.

Be Willing to Forgive Yourself

If you can't find a way to forgive yourself just yet, can you, at least, find the willingness to be willing to forgive yourself?

Where Are You Now?

How are you doing at forgiving yourself?

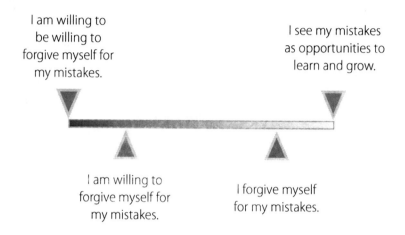

I am willing to be willing to forgive myself for my mistakes.

I see my mistakes as opportunities to learn and grow.

I am willing to forgive myself for my mistakes.

I forgive myself for my mistakes.

Once you get into the habit of forgiving yourself, you may want to go directly to:

"I forgive myself for _____."

Forgiveness Letter to Yourself

If you are not able to easily let go of something, you might write a forgiveness letter to yourself. Share it with another person, just as you did for anger and grief, and ask them to help you forgive yourself. S/he can act as a stand in forgiving you for the things you can't forgive yourself. "I forgive you for . . . ." This can be life-changing. Forgiving yourself allows you to accept yourself as you are, regardless of your past.

When you acknowledge yourself for all of who you are, you no longer need to put yourself down, hide yourself away, or cover up who you are. You accept yourself as human. There is more space in your heart for the important things—like love. This is an important aspect of turning point four.

As you write your letter, consider this question: What am I afraid will happen if I forgive myself?

Releasing the Charge

You can make the decision to forgive—and actively go about doing it—but still have conflicting feelings when you think of the person who hurt you. It doesn't necessarily mean you have not forgiven; it's just that there is some cleanup work to do. The following exercises will help you to get closer to experiencing the emotional release that comes with true letting go. Use any or all of them, and repeat as needed until the charge fades.

Releasing the Charge

■ Picture yourself holding the hurt in your hands. It may help to do this with an object that represents the hurt, for example a rock: cold, hard, and weighty. Literally, or in your mind's eye, release the hurt into a deep pool where it sinks lower and lower until it disappears from view. Proclaim it gone.

- When your car is particularly dusty or dirty, write a few words representing the transgression on the car. Wash it and watch the hurt run down the drain.

- Write the painful feelings down on paper and burn it.

- Picture the incident in your rearview mirror, and see it getting smaller and smaller as you distance yourself from it.

- Write it on a helium balloon and set it free.

- See the event in your mind's eye, and imagine turning a knob that allows you to soften the sound, dim the lights, and slow the motion on the scene until all is still and quiet.

- Make a list of at least ten traits you admire, or once admired, about your former partner, e.g., "he has beautiful eyes," "she is a good mother." Honoring what is good in another can elevate you from a hateful position to a kinder, gentler place, enabling you to let go more easily.

- After you've written your list, be still for a few moments. See your former mate in your mind's eye and send light, love, and good will. Their actions are their own and are no longer your concern.

Opportunities for Practice

After you've been away from your former partner for a while, it may throw you off balance when you accidentally cross paths. If you have children or still own your home or a business together, you may have these encounters more often than you would like. Even the thought of such an encounter may cause feelings of alarm.

Sometimes it's useful to play out a scenario in your head before it actually happens. Imagine seeing your former partner in a public setting, perhaps at your child's school event or the grocery store. See him or her walking toward you. Stay still and feel your response. Are you apprehensive? Do you remain calm? Is your stomach tight? Are you glad to see him or her? Are you angry? Are there tears? Do you want to run? Do you want to attack? Do you even care? Can you center yourself and find the calm inside rather than allow the circumstance to take you over?

You can use an encounter as a barometer of your success at forgiving or, more accurately, a barometer of how you are doing at creating a new life for yourself. Redesigning your life is turning point five. If you find that you are anxious, you know that you have more work to do, and you must continue to protect your heart while you heal. The time will come when seeing or not seeing your Ex won't matter anymore. When you have created a life for yourself that is calm, centered, loving, and purposeful, you won't care much about what s/he is doing. There is great freedom in this. Use these chance encounters as another marker along the path to gauging your recovery. If you can hang on to yourself while in your Ex's presence, you can be assured that you've let go and laid claim your own life.

Use your journal to log these chance encounters to see how you are progressing. Notice how your response changes over time. You can set it up like this:

Date: _____ Place: _____
Your response: _____

After forgiving and letting go, you may notice your Ex across a room and have no emotional charge whatsoever. Perhaps you will then truly wish the best for your former mate.

Does Forgiving Mean Getting Hurt Again?

A common concern about forgiving is the belief that forgiving means you must trust that person again, or that the relationship should resume right where it left off before you were hurt. "Forgive and forget" is what many of us were taught, but that is the opposite of what is actually helpful. It is important that you *not* trust again until you have solid evidence that the person can behave in a trustworthy manner. Knowing the difference between forgiving and trusting is important.

Forgiveness is about the past, and is freely given. You were hurt, you release the offender from the responsibility of fixing it. Trust, on the other hand, is about the future;

it must be earned. This is a tricky process that is often not available to divorcing couples, but I mention it here to help you understand how it differs from forgiveness.

You may never hear what you want to hear from the person who hurt you, either because the person is no longer living or the relationship is so damaged that the two of you aren't communicating. In either of those cases, forgiveness is your only option for setting yourself free. Remember, forgiveness is the gift you give yourself. You don't need the presence or permission of the other person in order to forgive. When you forgive in this way, you honor yourself and claim your dignity by taking the high road, which is a great boost to your self-esteem.

Sometimes, after awakening to the pain of his or her choice to leave the relationship, the Heartbreaker wants to reconcile. As the Heartbroken, you may be tempted to forgive them and accept. There are many important discussion points in my eBook *Should We Reconcile?* that will help you determine if this would be a good move.

How Will I Know I Have Forgiven?

This is a question I often hear. The simple answer is: You will know. If you're asking the question, you probably haven't— at least not as fully as you one day will. There is a lightness to forgiveness and a heaviness in non-forgiveness. You can feel it in yourself, and you can feel it in others.

The more complicated answer is that there are a number of more subtle indicators. One is your *thinking*. Which types of thoughts dominate? Do you relive the details of a betrayal over and over again? Are you consumed with what you should have said or done? Or, what your partner should have said or done? Or, on the other hand, do you think about how you can be the best parent, how to decorate your living space, find a job that suits you, or focus on your next creative endeavor? Non-forgiveness requires a tremendous amount of energy. When you are focusing your energy toward things you want to do instead of on your former partner, you will know you have reached a measure of forgiveness.

Another indicator is how you *feel*. We all have base-line emotions that I refer to as center line, as shown in the Line Chart of Emotions in the chapter on fear. There are positive, higher emotions above that line such as love, joy, and gratitude. There are also emotions below the line like despair, envy, and hate. Which emotions are present for you most of the time? Are they the more positive above-the-line emotions? Do you feel gratitude, optimism, and excitement? Do you trust that things are coming around? If so, you've moved into another level of forgiveness. Or, are they still below the line? Are you tense, afraid, reactive, blaming, a victim? Then you've got a ways to travel.

Remember that your feelings are yours, that they have a message for you, and it is up to you to take the appropriate action for their resolution. Forgiving isn't black and white as in "either you forgive or you don't." There are levels of forgiveness, and corresponding levels of freedom. If your movement is to the lighter emotions, you're making progress!

Where Are You Now?

How are you doing at forgiving your former partner?

Can't do it.

I'm Free!

I've chosen to
forgive but don't
feel relief yet.

25

Recovering Your Self-Worth

*Your ultimate goal in life is to
become your best self. Your immediate goal is to get on
the path that will lead you there.
The highest love a person can have for you is
to wish for you to evolve into the best person you can be.*

— DAVID VISCOTT, M.D., *THE LANGUAGE OF FEELINGS*

One of the benefits of being in a good relationship is that you have a champion in your corner. But when you split up, not only have you lost your champion, in many cases your former ally is actively undermining you. Without that source of validation, you may lose not only your self-esteem but your very identity. If you are no longer Jeremy's wife or Susie's husband or a keeper of the home or provider, who are you?

If your marriage was at least mostly positive, you may have arrived at the divorce door with strong self-esteem, however it is more likely that your relationship damaged your self-worth and divorce has magnified it. Good relationships aren't usually the ones that end.

Maybe you've added to your poor self-image by believing damaging words your Ex has spoken to you and about you. You let him or her deep into your heart because you trusted s/he would treat it kindly. But once there, s/he was able to do damage in ways that no one else could because you were vulnerable.

Rebuilding your self-worth is a many-layered process with each layer contributing, leading eventually to a sense of wholeness. Everything we cover in this book is intended to help you rebuild your self-worth, but this chapter is specifically devoted to it.

Let's review the ways to rebuild self-worth that we've covered so far.

- Accepting your emotions as normal and ultimately an ally in creating your new life
- Managing your thoughts, including how much you blame yourself
- Questioning the rules you live by
- Changing the lens through which you view yourself and life in general
- Challenging the authority of your inner critic
- Learning what went wrong so you can take charge and choose differently
- Forgiving—yourself and also your former partner
- Using boundaries to protect yourself and the things you care about

Each individual concept works together to bring you back to a strong sense of self. No doubt you are already feeling better than you were when you started this book. And there's more.

Reclaim Your Self-Worth to Rebuild Your Life

Two things are needed to regain self-worth. You must both stop participating in things that damage your self-worth, which I refer to as "stopping the bleeding," and make diligent effort to focus on things that will build you back up. When regaining physical health we must stop eating junk food and replace it with healthy food; for our mental health we must replace unhealthy thoughts and patterns with those that help us feel good about ourselves. Two big activities that bleed your self-worth are comparing yourself to your Ex or other divorcing people and losing sight of the positive aspects of life. Let's address each of them before we move on to suggestions for building your self-esteem to solid levels.

Stop the Bleeding: Comparison

Do you compare yourself to your Ex? Does it seem like the kids like him or her better? Is s/he doing better financially, or with a new love? Does it look like s/he has moved on, leaving you in the dust? Making these types of comparisons bleeds out your self-worth. Instead of keeping your energy close in order to create what you want, you're expending it on the person who likely deserves it the least. Isn't it time to take back your power?

When You Are Tempted to Compare

Keep track of the times and circumstances in which you compare yourself to your Ex. At the end of a day, review the list and next to each one write something that you do as well or better than your Ex. For example: If your Ex has more money to spend on the kids than you, note the heart-centered things you do with your kids.

Keep this up until you habitually respond to a negative comparison, whether with your Ex or someone else, with something you do well.

Stop the Bleeding: Losing Sight of the Positive

Have you lost sight of the positive aspects of your life situation? It's easy to do when there is a lot of negativity around you. We feel better about ourselves when we perceive things are going well. It's worth looking for the positives.

Love, joy, and happiness are giddy and fun emotions. When we experience them we feel light, as if all is well with the world. Despair, hopelessness, and loneliness are weightier, painful emotions. When we experience these, we feel the weight of the world. It is no wonder we are driven to pursue the things that make us happy in this life. Many of our emotions have a life of their own, showing up when they want to and staying as long as they want with little regard for our personal wishes. There is one of the high-frequency emotions, however, that we can use as leverage.

Gratitude for what we do have, and for what is going well, changes our perspective. Gratitude is a high-frequency emotion, and it is also an intellectual state. What I mean by that is that we can choose to focus on the things for which we are grateful. When we do, we notice more of them. Seeing the world through the lens of gratefulness is a new experience for many of us. I love the saying, "We don't see the world as it is. We see it as we are." That which we focus on tends to grow, whether we focus on things that are going well or things that make us miserable. It takes diligent moment-by-moment awareness to choose the positive.

A Gratitude Journal

One way to begin to move to higher-frequency emotions is to keep a gratitude journal. I suggest you keep a separate journal for this purpose. Once or twice a week, write about everything for which you are grateful. If things feel especially stressful, or if you feel especially grateful, you may want to write more often.

Start with simple things: a roof over your head, blue sky, a heart that beats. As you get more practice, you will notice more subtle things. Even the smallest things can bring a smile once you notice them: geese in the sky, a rosebud opening, the cold nose of a pet—all are there for the noticing. Being thankful for the emotional connection we have with friends releases oxytocin, the powerful feel-good hormone.

Rewriting Your Programming

In addition to putting a stop to the things that drain our sense of value, we can take proactive steps to rebuild our self-esteem. One way is to rewrite our programming. Life, and the people in it, has programmed your internal software since the day you were born. You learned about the world around you by internalizing the words and behaviors of others, especially as they related to you. We mimic those around us until we have enough of a sense of self that we don't need to do that any more. If things went well in childhood, the adults around you made the world safe. If you cried they held you. If you were hungry they fed you. This is the way we come to trust the world. When we were young it was our parent figures who had this influence; later it was peers.

We rewrite our software the same way we were programmed the first time, which is by internalizing, or letting in, outside messages. The difference now is that we can choose the source of those messages by choosing to listen only to people we trust.

We increase our self-esteem by surrounding ourselves with people who tell us the good they see in us by honestly reflecting our courage, kindness, integrity, parenting skill, fearlessness, and whatever else is true. I had the good fortune of attending life-coach training at the time of my divorce. My peers were kind but challenging supporters. It will serve you to have those supports, too.

While we don't want to be totally dependent on someone else to provide our sense of value, the fact is that other people play a big role in how we feel about ourselves. I have found that participants who hear positive messages about themselves during our face-to-face classes have been greatly impacted, but this is not as effective as hearing positive messages over time, under many conditions, from people you know. If your self-worth needs a major rewrite, you may want to get yourself into a group designed for that purpose. For now, you can do a similar exercise that we do in the live class.

Receiving Positive Messages

Think of five people who know you well and who would be willing to tell you what they love and admire about you. If you like, tell them that you are in a divorce recovery program and this is one of your assignments. Because this can be a difficult request initially, I have provided some suggested wording for you. You might include it in an email or speak your version of it on the phone to get the exercise started. Be sure to change it so it is just right for you. If you don't want to reveal that it's a divorce recovery program, that's fine. It won't make any difference in the end result.

"I am going through a [divorce recovery] program and have an assignment that you could help me with. [Because divorce is so hard on a person's self-esteem,] I am to ask supportive friends to tell me all the good, kind, affirming, courageous things

that they know to be true about me. Would you be willing? It will help me a lot to hear your words. I will receive them with gratitude. Thank you."

There are no rules other than for the comments to remain positive and affirming. The more comments you receive the better. It is best if your friends both speak them to you and write them down so you can read them later. Your job is to simply listen. *"You're a good friend." "I love your eyes." "I can't believe how brave you've been."* Receive the words as the gift that they are. Let the words sink into your heart. Your friends' words are an offering from their hearts to yours.

You may be tempted to throw the compliments back or deflect them in some way, such as *"I am not"* or *"Oh, but you do that so much better than I do."* Instead, be still and listen. Take it in. Allow yourself that gift. If you've received written copies, find a quiet place and read them in one sitting. Read each one slowly, letting the words sink in. After you have consciously taken in their kind and generous words, write down your thoughts. You might want to create an image board to capture how you feel after hearing all these wonderful things about yourself. You can copy and paste the words themselves into a collage or create a song or paint a picture using them. Make these words come alive for you in whatever way works.

After this initial reading, read them again every day and/or night for a week, and then, again, at any time you feel unheard or unloved. These people see and know your essence. Trust that.

The Good, the Bad, and the Ugly

Another way to build self-esteem is to reframe the way you perceive yourself. Take a lined paper and divide it into three columns. Label the columns "The Good," "The Bad," and "The Ugly."[16]

In the "Bad" column list things that you want to change. You may even vow periodically that you're going to change these things but don't seem to get around to it. This is the column for New Year's resolution kind of stuff: lose weight, attend anger management class, quit smoking, etc.

In the "Ugly" column, list things you don't like about yourself but can't change: wearing eyeglasses, thinning hair, your height, your age, cellulite, etc.

In the "Good" column, list your positive traits, talents, strengths, anything you do well. Go ahead; write them all. Don't hold back.

- When you've completed your lists, look at the "Bad" column closely. These are things you can change, though you may have to work at it. Which *one* of these can you work on immediately to make the largest impact on your self- esteem?

- Next, look at the "Ugly" column. These are things you believe you need to change about yourself in order to be loved, respected, or accepted. But the truth is, you deserve to be loved just as you are. There are likely people who love you even with those traits. Choose to let these go. Release the belief that these things make you lovable or unlovable. They don't.

- Now look at the "Good" column. These are the items that really matter. Spend the majority of your time thinking about and celebrating these traits of yours. Make them the focus of your life. You might choose one a day, or one a week, on which to focus and magnify.

A Spiritual Solution

Self-worth is ultimately gained when we feel deeply loved and accepted in the darkest parts of ourselves. We rarely risk showing those dark parts to other people because the chance of rejection is so high. Instead we put on a mask of happiness, goodness, or whatever we believe others want to see. If love comes at all, it is to the false image we've projected, and our hurting parts remain unloved. The very mask we've used for protection becomes a barrier to love.

The solution then is to focus on who you truly are, which is perhaps the most important aspect of turning point four. Consider instead that you are not a divorcing person, a loser, a bad parent, broke, or an emotional wreck. Those may be part of your life circumstances right now, but they aren't who you ARE. You are the thought of Love in form, an extension of All That Is. As such, you have access to all wisdom, knowing and strength. At your core you are bright and beautiful, creative, resourceful, and whole. None of the rest of it matters in the big scheme of things. Sometimes this rediscovery requires a process of remembering. Life gets in the way, causing us to forget our true nature. When you realize that you are valuable simply because you exist, life changes. You don't have to *do* anything to be loved. Perhaps you have always evaluated yourself by the things you do: being a good provider, cooking great meals, attending every school function, being a good friend. But the truth is, who you are is far more important than anything you will ever do.

Your path to the Source of Love and Supply will be uniquely your own. The Taoists call it That Which Cannot Be Named. To the Lakotah people it is Wakan Tanka, which means Sacred Spirit. Christian scripture talks about it being the root and ground of love, the love that passes understanding. It is worth seeking. I've known many divorcing people who seek (and find) Spirit for the first time in their lives. I'm not sure how people get through such a painful transition without that kind of support, but I have known people who do.

If you are open to it, you can connect with Spirit at a church, synagogue, temple, in nature, through prayer and meditation, present-moment awareness, balanced-body practices like yoga and tai chi, a variety of spiritual practices, the presence of other beings who have themselves found it, and other means. Don't be surprised when Spirit responds to your seeking. Finding your Source of Love and Supply, and the freedom and empowerment that it brings, is perhaps the greatest boost there is to your self-esteem. Don't miss this powerful solution to poor self-worth.

Where Are You Now?

How are you doing at taking responsibility for your self-worth?

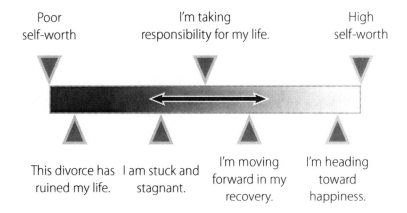

Poor
self-worth

I'm taking
responsibility for my life.

High
self-worth

This divorce has
ruined my life.

I am stuck and
stagnant.

I'm moving
forward in my
recovery.

I'm heading
toward
happiness.

Notice that self-responsibility is the tipping point between low and high self-worth. We feel helpless when someone or something other than ourselves is in charge of our life. It's empowering to take charge of our own happiness. Higher self worth and personal empowerment have a strong correlation.

26

Setting Effective Boundaries

The most important distinction anyone can ever make in their life is between who they are as an individual and their connection with others.

— ANNÉ LINDEN

N ow that you've learned about boundaries, what they are, what they protect, and when and how to use them, we turn to setting effective boundaries that will empower you while you are divorcing. Much of this chapter will focus on how to set effective boundaries with your Ex. But what you learn will help you in other areas of your life as well. One of the most powerful uses for boundaries while divorcing is unraveling the knots with your Ex so you can let go and move on.

Using Boundaries to Separate from Your Ex

Divorce means becoming separate individuals once again— not just partially, not with one foot in and one foot out of the relationship, but with completely separate lives. While you are divorcing, it may be hard to get used to the fact that you no longer have free access to your former partner, belongings that you once shared, or to the marital home you once lived in.

As one entity begins to divide into two, a space is created where boundaries are needed. It's no longer okay for your Ex to know everything you do or everyone you see. You may need to submit privacy paperwork so your former spouse no longer has access to your medical records. Your former partner may want to unload his or her emotions onto you, and you will need a boundary to assure that doesn't happen.

Whenever one of you sets a new boundary, it has the potential of setting off emotions in the other. It can feel like another loss or a major affront. It may incite strong anger while you come to grips with the fact that things are indeed changing. Even after you are divorced, learning that your former mate is dating may trigger a strong desire to know who they are seeing. It may feel like betrayal or infidelity even though the marriage is over.

Being a completely free individual, though perhaps hard to get used to at first, is empowering. This is turning point number four. You become the prime mover in your life, and those who want to be in relationship with you must rise to the standards you hold for yourself.

Three Layers of Separation

Separating isn't a simple thing. Besides all of the day-to-day schedules and *things* that must be separated, there are deep levels of entwinement that must be released also. We don't usually think of separating on more than a physical level, but as anyone who has tried and failed to cut ties after repeated attempts knows, there is more to it than physical separation. In order to become completely free individuals once again, separation must take place on three levels:

1. The tangible day-to-day level—house, home, cars, time, money, etc.
2. The dreaming level—your hopes, dreams, and goals for a future together.
3. An essence or soul/heart level—the emotional oneness, intimacy, and chemistry between you.

You can remain connected on one, two, or all three levels. For example, you may be entwined on a heart level (essence) still entertaining a future together (dreaming), but be glad to live in a different house (tangible). Your partner may have stopped dreaming about any kind of future, feel no connection on the heart level, but be okay sharing the home together until it sells. When the two of you are entwined on different levels, it adds to the confusion.

You became entwined in these levels over time. Maybe you moved in together with the hopes that future dreams and intimacy would develop. Maybe you had a lot of chemistry, were very connected on the essence/intimacy level, but could never really make it work in the tangible day to day.

Although the severing can happen in any order, for one partner it may start with the realization that his or her dreams have changed. For the other partner it may not become real until it manifests at the tangible level. There is something about seeing the furniture go out the door that makes the reality hard to deny.

It often takes a while for couples to disentangle on the heart (essence) level. It can be confusing when the two of you are living separately (disentangled on the day-to-day level) and no longer dream of a future together (disconnected on a dreaming level), but remain hooked in the undercurrent of the essence level by a force unseen but definitely felt. This is the root of many post-divorce legal battles, which my attorney friends tell me are fairly prevalent, and often more difficult, than the original divorce.

Boundaries have an important role in disentangling on the three levels. Each partner will set limits in the areas where they feel most complete. The partner who is disentangled on the heart and dreaming levels may forbid their partner to talk about wanting to be together or still being in love. *"I don't want to hear it. We're done."* The partner who is glad to be physically separated may have strong boundaries around the former mate showing up at the door unannounced.

To avoid sending conflicting messages, you will want to make your boundaries consistent on all three levels. Having sex with your soon-to-be Ex will keep you entangled on the essence level. Talking of a shared future, even if it is just friendship, will keep you entangled on the dreaming level. Anyone who has shared a home with their soon-to-be Ex knows how difficult it is to be in the same physical space.

Fear of Setting Limits

It is hard to set limits on someone you still need, no matter how crazy he or she is making you. Darlene's need was financial. She and Jake were divorcing but still living in the same house. He was having an affair and refused to stop seeing the woman. He wanted the divorce and, given the circumstances, Darlene did too. The situation got even more complicated when Jake developed a medical condition that required constant care. If anything happened to Jake, Darlene would be in poverty. He was the sole support for both of them. She chose to take care of him so the mistress wouldn't be in their home, even though taking care of a man who no longer loved her and was actively betraying her, caused her so much harm.

Darlene needed outside support to get her out of that debilitating situation. She needed other people who could help her stand up for herself and to see other options. As long as she needed Jake so desperately she couldn't set those important limits. Maybe your partner has a similar hook to reel you in for the umpteenth time. You can take away his or her leverage by having support in other places. If your former partner has been your sole source of support, it will be difficult to impossible to set necessary limits. It feels a little like cutting your sole lifeline.

If you were in the child position in your relationship, you are particularly susceptible to boundary violations and being taken advantage of. You may need financial support, emotional support, and support with daily tasks. You've not had the same opportunities to learn what you need in order to become more independent. Maybe you are hearing something like, *"I'm going to cut off the credit card,"* or *"I won't let you see the kids,"* or *"I won't pay child support."* There are many other versions. If you need legal support, get it. (For low-cost legal help, search online for legal services and/or the bar association for your county. If you need immediate help, find a local shelter. Even if you don't need the housing part of it -the shelter may have many other resources, many of them free.) You should not be left destitute, deprived of seeing your children, or in physical danger. Temporary Orders through the court system should help you with immediate needs until details can be worked out during your divorce. A restraining order can protect you, your property, and your kids if that's needed. Talk to an attorney about your options. Most attorneys provide what they call unbundled legal services. You don't have to hire them to represent you, but you can gain their legal advice for an hourly fee.

We have two basic fears that cause us to not set important limits. As relational beings we don't want to be shunned or seen as selfish and end up alone, and we don't want to incite anger and be attacked. Too many people have a painful history as the result of standing up for themselves. If you are afraid, you will put up with more hurtful things than someone with more resources. *"I know s/he treats me badly, but at least I'm not alone,"* you may say to yourself. Being with people who remind you of your worth will help you develop and hold to your boundaries when those fears arise.

Everyone is born with the ability to set boundaries, but if your boundaries were ignored or overridden, or if you were talked out of them, disciplined out of them, or had love withdrawn because of them, you may have learned to deny them. I hope you will let your divorce experience inspire you to relearn protective boundaries. Personal empowerment is turning point four.

Enforcing Boundaries

There are consequences for entering another person's property uninvited. Signs warn: *Trespassers Will Be Prosecuted!* You must enforce your limits with promised actions or they will be seen merely as empty threats. Enforcement means setting a limit with stated consequences and following through. Be prepared to change your plans if you need to in order to enforce your boundaries. For example, *"We've agreed that you'll pick up the kids at 4:00. If you aren't there and you haven't called, we are leaving."* This may be hard if you have to be at work by 5:00. You will learn when you need a backup plan.

Even during his divorce, Jeremy still took care of everything he could. He wanted his kids to have a good home, so he took care of refinancing the family home that would belong to his ex-wife Kate. He waited and waited and waited for her to complete her financial papers. Months turned into years, and nothing changed. He'd met someone else and was pursuing that relationship, but was still married to Kate. His inability to set limits with Kate created a very sticky situation for all of them.

Once he realized that setting stronger limits with Kate was *for* him and not *against* her, he changed strategies. He consulted his attorney to determine his legal leverage and told her, "If you don't have the financial papers completed by _____, then I will have to _____." He could have forced movement in his divorce years earlier if he'd known this important skill.

On the flip side of this, boundaries are not a one-way street to serve only you. You will also need to accept logical and legitimate boundaries set by your Ex. Getting mad when we don't get our way is counterproductive and immature. As best you can, observe your Ex's boundaries without taking them personally. Your Ex also has a self to protect and may be new at it, just like you. It is rare that one person in the relationship is great at boundaries and the other knows nothing. Knowing that your Ex is learning, too, may help you be more forgiving and cooperative. His or her boundary is not necessarily *against* you, but may very well be just *for* him or her. It may not feel good to honor your Ex's boundaries but by doing so, you can reduce a lot of the friction between you as you take this important step toward living separate lives.

You'll also want to consider the impact of laying down hard boundaries, particularly concerning finances and parenting time. This can generate deep fears in your soon-to-be Ex. It serves no one. The truth is, only in unusual circumstances will the courts allow a big discrepancy in the financial resources or parenting time allotted to each.

Better to hear your partner's fears and try to meet them than try to beat them with hard boundaries.

If you need extra support to understand the importance of, and your right to, have boundaries, consider getting help from a therapist who can help you reclaim your right to yourself.

When Setting Boundaries Is Complicated

The combination of desperately needing to have distance between you, alongside the necessity of having to work together to get through the divorce process, and parent together after, can be very trying. Having clear boundaries will protect your heart and your time during this delicate period.

Ginny experienced this. She and her soon-to-be-Ex had major battles while meeting with the mediator and yet still spent time together with their grown children, acting as if everything was fine. They participated in a week-long camping vacation with their children and mates, and the grandchildren. Without special boundaries like separate tents and the agreement not to discuss anything about the divorce while on the vacation, it could have been a difficult situation for everyone.

Boundaries for the Digital Age

As if divorce isn't complicated enough, in our modern world we must also disentangle from the many ways we are connected online. We must separate not only physically, emotionally, and socially, but also digitally.[17]

Facebook can be a happy place with a new community of friends, but the last person you want to see your updates is your Ex. You may want to share aspects of your divorce and new life without considering who is seeing your posts. And do you really want to hear about your Ex's grand social life when you're sitting at home alone? It's okay, and probably wise, to unfriend your former spouse. Facebook provides a way to block people so that neither you, nor they, see anything about the other in posts of mutual friends or family.

LinkedIn is an online professional network. Even though less personal information is shared than on Facebook, if you stay "linked" you will be apprised of your Ex's updates.

Depending on how involved you are in the technology world you may have to disconnect in other ways, also. Foursquare is a geo-location check-in game, allowing you to let friends know where you are. Those who are near can then drop by to visit. If you don't want your former partner to know you are at the local pub at 2 A.M., you may want to disconnect there, too. Consult the "Help" section of any of these websites to learn how to unhook.

Email is an aspect of technology we all have to manage, especially while divorcing. Any email related to your divorce has the potential to be bad news that may highjack your happiness. At work it can ruin your productivity. At home it can interfere with precious alone time or time with your kids. The computer lurking in the corner with the potential for bad news can put a pall over your new living space. Even when you're out and about, an untimely email can interrupt your social life if you have a smartphone. Just about every email program has a way to create a smart folder using "rules" or a filtering system. You can funnel emails from your Ex, divorce professionals, bill collectors, and the like directly into their own folder for later viewing. Again, the help section will show you how.

You may not initially know all the ways you need to disconnect digitally. Just take care of them as they reveal themselves. Remember that these boundaries are *for* you, to protect your heart, time, and other things we've been talking about.

Tending to Your Own Yard

Many divorcing people discover that they've taken on the responsibility for their partner's happiness. Realizing they are tired and that all their efforts haven't made their partner any happier, they quit. This can seem like a cold and ruthless act, but it may actually be a gift for both. The tired partner gets to put down that misplaced responsibility and focus on him/herself. The cared-for partner then takes up the cause of finding happiness within, which is where it has been all along. There are many other versions of this scenario.

If others are used to your being in charge of their happiness or taking care of them in other ways, they will not like you taking this off your plate. It will seem unloving, perhaps to both of you. When you give this responsibility back to them, be prepared for some flack. Setting up a boundary acts like a deflector. Your former partner's happiness, laziness, or mean spirit boomerangs back where it belongs, which is in his or her yard, and maybe for the first time in their lives they get to look at their own issues. It may be frightening for them and useful for you to be empathetic and understanding toward this part of their journey. You can be empathetic without making it about you.

Identify Your Boundaries

Below is a list of common boundaries that are often needed while divorcing. Identify those that would be useful to you right now. What support do you need to enforce your boundaries?

- **Communicate with your Ex only in writing and/or brief phone calls.** Keep all communication limited to only what is necessary for the kids or legal matters.

- **Hang up or walk away.** Let your Ex know that s/he must speak to you in respectful ways or the conversation is over. If s/he starts to speak to you in inappropriate ways, stop the conversation and hang up or walk away.

- **Keep your conversations business-like.** Do not discuss your fears, concerns, or personal issues because that only maintains the emotional tie between the two of you. Don't talk about anything that opens the door to more emotional entanglement.

- **Do not involve the children in any communication between the two of you.** Don't send messages through the kids. Keep them protected.

- **Don't allow your Ex to depend on you for support.** It's easy to fall into the "husband" or "wife" role again because it's habit. You don't need to be an emotional support for him. You don't need to fix her screen door. You are not there to assist as you did when you were married. You may develop a friendship later, but during divorce your job is to disentangle.

- **Protect your privacy.** You don't need to know where she goes, what she does, what she is thinking, or whom she is seeing . . . and she doesn't need to know those things about you either.

- **Your financial situation is private.** Consider your child support or maintenance (alimony) your money. Either the two of you agreed to it, or the court ordered it. It's yours. Your former spouse doesn't have the right to comment upon or berate you about finances. If you have problems with support checks, talk to your lawyer. Never beg or put yourself in an inferior position.

- **Have clear boundaries with your in-laws.** Do you want them in your life because you value that relationship or because you want to keep tabs on your Ex? Why do they want you in their lives? Be clear about what you expect.

■ **Make your home *your* home.** It is not his home. It is not a place to hang out with the kids. When she is in your house she is a houseguest like any other. A houseguest doesn't enter without knocking, raid the refrigerator, open cupboard doors, or remove pictures from the walls.

Where Are You Now?

Where are you in the boundary progression?

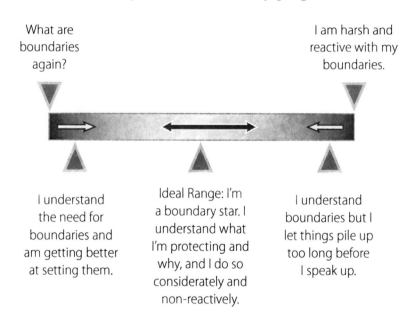

What are boundaries again?

I am harsh and reactive with my boundaries.

I understand the need for boundaries and am getting better at setting them.

Ideal Range: I'm a boundary star. I understand what I'm protecting and why, and I do so considerately and non-reactively.

I understand boundaries but I let things pile up too long before I speak up.

Part Seven

FUTURE RELATING

27

Your Relationship with Yourself

However I look and sound, whatever I say and do,
and whatever I think and feel at a given
moment in time is authentically me.
If later some parts of how I looked, sounded,
thought, and felt turn out to be unfitting,
I can discard that which is unfitting, keep the rest,
and invent something new for that which I discarded.

— VIRGINIA SATIR

I consistently hear two things from the divorced people I've worked with. They are at first compelled to be in a relationship again and it can't come soon enough. The vulnerability of being alone is too much. *"I've always been married. That's just who I am. I don't know how to be single."* The second thing I hear comes six months to a year beyond their divorce. The same person who didn't think they could survive outside marriage is now not only relieved to be single, they wouldn't trade the single life they have grown to love.

When you know who you are and stand powerfully in that, you stop harm before it gets to you, you attract people and situations that feed your soul, you can better discern what is good for you and what isn't, you know a safe person when you see one, and if you do happen to get fooled you bounce back more quickly than in the past. Knowing yourself and standing up for yourself are important aspects of the fourth turning point.

An important part of having a strong sense of self is developing a great singleness. That is one reason I recommend a rest period of a couple of years before dating in a serious way again. If you are like most people I talk with, your heart just dropped at the thought of waiting two years to date. That doesn't mean you must sit on your hands and do nothing. This time doesn't have to be idle at all. Use this time to rediscover yourself, to develop some great friendships. You have changed since your divorce. Values change, friendships change, and of course all that is involved in day-to-day living has changed. You need some time to settle into the new you. When you know who you are and what you want, you have a much better chance at creating a meaningful relationship in the future. Dating for fun can be part of learning about yourself. There are benefits and pitfalls in what I call transitional relationships. We will talk about those.

The Renaissance Period

Before we talk more about self-discovery, I want to tell you about a special period of time post-divorce. I've come to call it The Renaissance Period. When you meet someone who is in it, it is unmistakable. They glow. A door to opportunities once only dreamt suddenly appears. Those who walk through it become giddy at the possibilities before them. Where to begin? This is The Renaissance Period. This door opens after the divorce is final, when the emotions are mostly resolved, and the new beginning is clearly in view. The door can't open before that because your creative energy is still tied up in divorce details. But when it opens, it opens broadly. It's even a little scary at first. It takes some courage, and you need to allow yourself permission to walk through it.

Renaissance people dream as they haven't, sometimes, since they were children. When they realize it really is okay to feel good again, they set out with gusto to accomplish things they once thought lost to them—hobbies, adventures, expressing hidden talents. Maybe they dance, sing, write poetry, take to running marathons, play an instrument, jump out of an airplane, get their doctorate, wear a kilt, or ride a Harley. (Yes, I've known divorcing people who have done all of those things during their Renaissance Period.)

Renaissance people are feisty. They claim who they are without apology. They try out new relational skills, practice assertiveness, and proudly wear their newfound self-worth. They give their creative passion free rein. There's a new purpose to be had. I hope that when this door opens for you, you step through it with great fanfare.

As your painful emotions start to resolve you may find that they are replaced by a voracious hunger to learn, to understand, to continue the journey of personal growth you've begun. Follow that hunger. It will lead you to the doorway. Walk through that doorway and you find that you are face to face with the final turning point—designing your life anew.

Maybe you don't know where to begin to learn about yourself, so let me give you some ideas. (Please note that if the majority of your answers have something to do with being in a romantic relationship again, it may not be the right time for you to do this exploration. You may want to revisit this when you are further along in your process.)

Defining Yourself

Here are a few questions to help with your inner exploration. Take some time to write the answers to one or more of the questions in your journal, or talk to a friend about them.

1. What accomplishments or measurable events must occur for you to feel you've lived a satisfying and meaningful life?

2. If you looked in the dictionary under your name, what would it say?

3. Talk about two or three people who inspire you, and say why.

4. What do you feel so strongly about that no one can change your mind?

5. What is missing from your life, the presence of which would make it more fulfilling?

6. Imagine yourself at 80 years old surrounded by friends and family who have gathered to honor you for the impact you've made on their lives. Who is there and what do they say?

Who Am I Now?

Take a piece of lined paper and make two columns with these headings:

I like, I will, I want, I am . . .	I don't like, I won't, I don't want, I am not . . .

As you go about your day, make your lists. Many of your items will be paired opposites: "I like Chinese food. I don't like Mexican food." But they don't have to be: "I will allow Sam to help me with my taxes." "I won't allow Susan to make fun of the clothes I wear."

Defining yourself in this way begins to create a container to hold the new you. Your new identity may seem fragile or unformed at first, but as you identify who you are and then show up in life that way, your identity will become more solid. And as that identity becomes more real, you will naturally want to create a life to fit this person who is now familiar to you. This is how turning point four feeds into point five. Be aware that a lot of your identity lies at the edge of your comfort zone. I hope you won't shy away from stretching out there to find it.

Creating a Single Life You Love

Are you satisfied with how you connect with others, pick friends, handle crises, set goals and keep them, make decisions, and react in emotional situations? If not, here's your chance to change it. Crisis doesn't change who we are; it reveals us to ourselves. Divorce has given you a gift by pointing to the places where your life wasn't working. You now have the opportunity to change things around to something better. **Your life has been handed lovingly back to you.**

Stepping fully into your life will do a lot toward replacing loneliness. Loneliness is not as much about being alone as it is about waiting for others to create life for you, or with you. Once you take the reins you will feel empowered and wonder why you allowed loneliness to run things for so long. This equips you for the fifth turning point.

You will know you have a healthy singleness when your work life is in order, your finances are stable, you have a community of supportive friends, you are taking care of your health, you have a home that you feel comfortable in, and are—at least mostly—content with who you are. Although most of us want eventually to be in another meaningful relationship, having a fulfilling life as a single is a great reward in and of itself. A good singleness is far better than a bad relationship. Feeling good about ourselves allows us to enjoy life even without a partner. And isn't it interesting that so many people find that when they are content with their lives love shows up? It's one of life's ironies.

Where Are You Now?

To heck with being single. I want somebody, anybody, now.

I've learned about myself. I have a great bunch of friends. I'm ready to date again.

I'm not good at being alone. Even though I want to be in a relationship, I'm going to learn how to be happy on my own first.

28

Transitional Relationships

Living with integrity means:
Not settling for less than what you know
you deserve in your relationships.
Asking for what you want and need from others.
Speaking your truth, even though it
might create conflict or tension.
Behaving in ways that are in harmony
with your personal values.
Making choices based on what you believe,
and not what others believe.

— BARBARA DE ANGELIS

Most everyone is lonely after a divorce. We long for companionship, somebody to do things with on the weekend, or to call with good news. Sometimes we find buddies or girlfriends. Sometimes family fills this role. We may pay someone to listen as with a therapist or coach. Most of us realize we aren't ready for a romantic relationship so soon after divorce, but the loneliness is powerful and finding someone new to fill this role seems like an obvious solution. What do you need to consider?

Rebound or Transitional?

Most of us have heard of a rebound relationship. It is a do-over, a repeat, almost like a mini-marriage. There isn't a lot of choosing, but more a falling into relationship with the first willing person with whom you feel comfortable. There may be a feeling that this new person is perfect for you, having many good traits your Ex lacked, and none of the bad ones. There is hope that "this is the one." Many people don't want to get involved in this kind of relationship because they know they don't often turn out well. Others feel compelled despite the risks. Either they don't believe the stories or their need to be close with another person is so strong they are willing to take the chance.

Transitional relationships are somewhat different. They are more about exploring and growing and trying out new ways of relating. This works especially well if the other person is learning and growing, too. You've developed a hunger to sort things out, try new things, learn, grow, discover, to practice being yourself. It's an important step to practice those things in relationship. Deep honesty is important. A transitional relationship provides a place for thoughtful discussions about topics like the purpose of life, your hopes, dreams, and plans for the future.

A transitional relationship can provide a strong support during yet another in-between period in the divorce pro-cess—the period between the intense emotional upheaval and a serious dating relationship. There are some inherent pitfalls involved that you might want to be aware of. The most common pitfalls that I see are becoming attached too quickly, and trying to stretch a temporary relationship into something permanent.

Becoming Attached

Even though you have every intention of entering a new relationship lightly, perhaps just for companionship, your heart may get strongly attached because it's been broken and beaten and wants a little loving. You may find yourself dreaming of a future with someone you know very little about. Because of our needs, the attachments we feel can run deep. Many people confuse these strong feelings with love. It *feels* like what we imagine love to be.

When we put our emotions all in this one basket so to speak, we are vulnerable to the other person's whims and the flip-flopping nature inherent in these relationships.

Hanging On

These relationships are called transitional because they fill a gap—the gap between your old life and your new one. The gap between the person you were in your last relationship, and the person you are becoming. Transitional relationships are time-limited by nature. People come into our lives for a reason, a season, or a lifetime. We don't know which it is until it plays out. This special person may be a rest stop on a long journey that, for you, continues on alone. We cause ourselves double hurt by trying to make a relationship that is, by design, temporary into something lasting. We stretch it beyond normal limits and it may snap back forcefully. You may save yourself some heartache if you hold the possibility that this special relationship will likely end one day. To prevent more heartache as much as you can, enjoy it for what it is without expectation for a future.

Staying Flexible in a Transitional Relationship

The most important criteria for a successful transitional relationship is ongoing dialogue about fears, needs, wants, and expectations. You will want to negotiate the amount of time you spend together, whether to be sexual or not, when to involve your respective children, your changing attitudes about commitment, and maybe even an exit plan.

A transitional relationship has an entirely different frame than a lasting relationship. Long-term relationships need stability and commitment to make them work. Transitional relationships need flexibility and freedom to move. The purpose of a transitional relationship is companionship, healing, and self-discovery. You are changing, trying new things, new behaviors, you don't want to have to take care of someone else. You need the freedom to invest in yourself.

Your relationship values will continue to evolve as you do. Only when you are grounded in a solid sense of self are you ready to find a more permanent match. Dating while you are in a state of flux will bring you dates who are also in flux in their own lives. This can be a good thing. You wouldn't want Mr. or Ms. Right to come along before you are ready.

Learning from Your Transitional Relationships

If you've worked the steps in this book, you've learned a lot about yourself and likely identified some things you want to do differently in future relationships. Here are some ideas for things to practice:

- If you felt controlled in your last relationship, use your boundary-setting skills.
- If you were a caretaker, allow yourself to be loved and cared for. Say "no" once in a while.
- If you were passive, own your feelings and express them openly.
- If you've taken charge of the happiness of others, focus on your happiness instead.
- If you are over-responsible, let go of control and your need to be seen as perfect. Let the other person decide where to eat or what movie to watch.
- If you have been under-responsible, practice being powerful. Take charge of yourself.

What other behaviors would you like to practice?

You can also practice skills like open and honest communication, taking emotional risks to find a workable balance of safety and vulnerability, discerning the line between being loving and caretaking, finding the balance between speaking your needs and being aware of the needs of the other, staying present, taking one day at a time, avoiding projecting yourself and the relationship into an imagined future, and the often-forgotten skill of having fun and not being so serious, lost, or downhearted.

This relationship may feel different—more alive, honest, real—than the relationship you had with your Ex, or maybe any relationship you've ever had. It's easy to believe it is because of this new person you are with, but the truth is it's different because *you* are different. It's exhilarating to finally be yourself.

Conscious Endings

Relationships change. We are growing and evolving beings so it fits that our relationships will grow and evolve with us . . . or they won't. When they don't, or when they've outlived their usefulness, it is time to move on. If you've made conscious agreements during the developmental phase of your transitional relationship, it may still hurt when it ends, but it doesn't have to devastate you. If you've been attentive to what you've learned in this book, you've gotten stronger; you've learned how to take care of yourself; your self-worth has improved; you've had some practice with boundaries; you have skills to deal with the grief and anger, guilt and loneliness; you've paid more attention to warning signs; you've not risked more than you could afford to lose. You've built a foundation of open communication and practiced being yourself. Most importantly, you've built a support community and a single life you love so you aren't captive to your transitional relationship for support.

When it is time to end your transitional relationship, it will likely involve a tough conversation. Here are some things you might say or hear:

- My feelings are changing.
- I no longer enjoy the things we do together.
- I'm starting to feel confined.
- I realize I didn't really find myself after my divorce.
- I'm holding you back.
- I'm starting to feel like I'm married again.
- I don't know what I want.
- You expect too much from me.
- I don't want to be in this relationship any more.

If you can have an open and honest conversation about your changing feelings, it may still hurt when it ends (that is natural when we've invested our hearts), but it doesn't have to wreck you. You can get with your supportive friends, use the skills you've learned, cry as much as you need to, move through the In-Between Zone and on to the next iteration of yourself, just like you did before. You will still experience the emotions, but this time you know more about what to expect and you have supportive people who can hold you up while you let down. The important question you will eventually come to once again is, *What is it time to let go of?*

When it's time to end, it may seem easier to just fade away, to quit calling, to not show up—to say/email/text that it's over and disappear, but that is just cowardly. It creates hurt and resentment. You two have been important to each other and talking it through is also important. It's far worse to avoid the conversation. Both of you need to express, be heard, and be acknowledged. Taking ownership of your part in the ended relationship is also an empowering step for you. It's part of claiming your new values.

Depending on the depth of your involvement in the day to day, you may need to also talk about important topics like how you will tell your friends, who will live where, separating finances, child visitation, and pets. If it seems appropriate you might want to talk about what you want your relationship to look like in six months, a year, five years. I provide a non-legal separation agreement on my website that may help you with that discussion.

On the other hand, if it looks like you are going to be together for a while, you will likely want to learn more about the stages of relationship and begin the study of what makes relationships work. I can direct you to important resources.

29

Loving Again

Don't say you love me unless you mean it
because I might do something stupid . . . like believe it!

— Unknown

A lmost every divorcing person I talk with wants eventually to be in a loving relationship again, as long as it can be different/better than the one they left. They'd put a lot of hopes and dreams into a relationship that didn't work out. The marriage ended but the hopes and dreams did not. Loneliness is a powerful motivator. Perhaps it is so strong that you feel compelled to find new love. Maybe the thought of facing the future alone is overwhelming. The security you once had about the future is gone and you want it back. There are many reasons for pursuing love again. In this chapter we will explore the most common and look at some of the joys and pitfalls of seeking new love.

Complete the Old Relationship

As said earlier, it is common to think that new romance is the solution to loneliness and other leftover ailments from divorce. But the truth is, you can never replace a lost lover. You can only build love again with a new person. Your first step is to complete the emotional business around your old relationship. If you don't, you will have a hole in your heart in the shape of your Ex and try to fit new loves into that hole. When that new love doesn't fit, you will either subconsciously decide they aren't the right one or you may stick it out in a continual state of disappointment because they aren't meeting your needs, never realizing you have a hidden ideal you are measuring against. Indeed, it may be hidden even to you. Trying to fit a new person into an old mold, or comparing them to both the good and bad traits of your Ex, will just make you both miserable. Heartache and discouragement are inevitable outcomes.

Be aware (or is that "beware"?) that any incomplete business, whether that is resentment, grieving, neediness, or the like, will come back to haunt you in your future relationships. Dating before you've completed the emotional business around your past relationship almost guarantees that you will choose the same kind of person you just left. In the big picture, relationships are here to teach us. If we don't learn the lessons the first time, they will show up again and again until we get it. I hope that statement is sobering.

To Date or Not to Date

How do you feel about dating again? (Even though *dating* is a rather outdated term, I'll use it here to refer to the process of getting to know someone with the purpose of seeing if they are a fit for a long-term partnership.) Do you long to date again? Are you terrified at the thought of it? Are you taking "me" time and not interested in dating right now? Most divorcing people have a tug-of-war going on inside them. One side of the war is a strong desire to be in a loving relationship again. The other side of the war is near terror at the thought of what it will take. And of course there is the ever-present nagging doubt . . . "What if I don't find love again?" Both of those drives may live simultaneously in your head and your heart, causing you to feel stuck. Staying where you are is not an option, but you don't have the confidence to go forward either. This stuckness points to the need for further healing. As you continue to heal, the terror will subside. If you're still afraid, you're really not ready, despite what your friends and family may tell you. "Just get back out there" is not sound relationship advice. This is the period of time that I call the "cootie" stage. Remember when you were young and the opposite sex had cooties? You weren't supposed to be interested in them romantically, and you likely aren't supposed to be interested in them right now, either.

A dating relationship is one of the least safe relationships in which to risk your heart. Many divorcing people want to date because they want to soothe their hurts, but bringing a wounded child-heart—and that is often the part in us that hurts the most—to a relationship that is, by design, filled with rejection, is a recipe for heartbreak.

Before you venture into the dating scene, here are some questions to consider:

- Are you aware of your past dysfunctional relationship patterns? Do you have a plan for avoiding them? Have you made some effort to heal them?

- Do you know which part of you is doing the seeking? (the wise part, the lonely part, the horny part, the financially insecure part, as examples)

- Do you know your personality strengths and weaknesses?

- How stable are you in the important life areas like career, parenting, finances, health, and housing?

- Do you have a personal vision for your life going forward?

- Do you know your requirements, needs, and wants for a future relationship?

- Have you thought about what you want to learn about yourself as you date?

- How are your boundary skills? Can you protect things that are important to you, including your heart, while you date?

Beware of Sharks

Many people experience a period of what can only be called insanity as their divorce begins to resolve. Driven by loneliness, poor self-image, lack of feeling grounded, and fueled by newfound freedom, you may watch yourself participate in behaviors you know are out of control, somewhat like a teen who has lived with controlling parents and when off to college realizes there is a whole world of sex, drugs, and rock and roll out there. "Driven" is an apt description. After experiencing this newfound freedom many find a powerful sex drive they'd lost, or never had, in their unhappy marriage. It often surprises people who have had zero sex drive for years to suddenly experience it so powerfully. Growing up has a lot of surprises.

A friend described this period in his divorce as being adrift on a raft in shark-infested waters. The sharks are self-damaging behaviors like falling in "infatuation" too soon; excessive sex, alcohol, drugs, over-spending, and non-existent self-care. The sharks themselves may not seem so harmful, but the bite will get your attention. The bites are things like an unwanted pregnancy, STDs, addictions, financial or health problems, and hits to your self-esteem.

Going afloat on these waters is an attempt to feel loved and good about yourself again; you are driven by unmet needs. Loneliness is a huge driver at this time. You may snap out of it from time to time, like when a friend grabs you by the collar and you realize you're doing yourself more harm than good. But how do you stop? It all feels so necessary. You may deeply believe that you need romantic love to feel good again, but that is a misnomer. You need love. Absolutely. But there are safer and more effective places to get it this soon after divorce.

Many of our deepest needs, which when unmet contribute to the loneliness we feel, developed early in life. They are pre-sexual. To heal them you will need to allow yourself to be loved in non-romantic, non-sexual, relationships so you can fill your love tank. You don't want to be running on empty in the dating world. That is a setup for experiencing some really bad, perhaps even abusive, behavior with a little heartbreak thrown in on the side.

Sexual Again?

When to be sexual again is a deep question with far-reaching implications. This section will touch on the aspects most important to people right after divorce. I have a personal bias toward getting to know yourself and the other person well before being sexual. Although I have included other possibilities, I am recommending what I've learned provides the best results for the most people while protecting them from the most hurt.

People have the same concerns about being sexual as they do for dating, only more intensely. Some people want to be sexual again immediately. Some don't want anything to do with it. If sex in their marriage was deeply unsatisfying or abusive, there is often a drive to be sexual again to heal. Sexual feelings after divorce can be very powerful.

As our social lives and sense of community have become more disconnected, we have become more dependent on our primary relationships to feel connected. Sex is being asked to fill a need it was never intended to fill. Many people believe that if they have a sexual relationship they are loved and may seek one sexual relationship after another, hoping for the love they never had or lost along the way. They may find it, but often not.

The decision to be sexual again is a weighty one. Your approach to sexuality is the same as any decision, but with potentially greater consequences. We've all made stupid decisions in our youth. We can make some potentially bad decisions while divorcing, too. Here are some questions for you to consider.

- Have you identified your long-term relationship goals? Does being sexual at this time fit with those goals?

- Will you still be happy with what you've chosen when you are past this crazy post-divorce period?

- Which part of you is making the choice? The fearful part? Lonely part? Horny part? Rebellious part? What would your most resourceful self choose?

- Do you think having sex would give you energy or drain it away? Would you love yourself more, or less? Be stronger? Feel used? Ask the same questions about not having sex. What is needed to make it a good experience?

- How might your choice affect children who are watching for your example and guidance?

- And ultimately, how will you handle someone getting attached to you, or you getting attached to them, or a pregnancy, or an STD?

How was it to answer those questions? If you haven't considered these types of questions, you might want to spend some more time getting to know yourself before you risk your heart so deeply, as in a sexual relationship.

Head, Heart, or Hormones?

A broken heart is hard enough to heal when there's no sex involved and excruciatingly long and painful when it is. Sex creates an attachment that wouldn't otherwise be there because of the release of oxytocin and other feel-good hormones. The hormonal bath your brain experiences during sex is hard to undo. It is chemistry, in the literal sense of the word, and making an intellectual decision not to get attached is overridden. Being under the influence of those chemicals can cause you to make deeply wrong relational choices, or to stay in a relationship that isn't good for you. Basically, your brain is tricked. Just knowing that may help you avoid some painful discoveries.

It will serve you to balance your heart with your head. I've talked to dozens of people who've held very specific intentions to remain non-sexual only to find that when presented with the opportunity, they are ill-prepared for the intensity. The drive for connection, the desire to feel loved, the fear of that love going away, or that it may never come around again, and lonely nights all work together and undermine their best intentions. The loneliness wins. Sometimes it's immediately apparent that being sexual under those conditions, at that time, or with that person, wasn't the best idea. Sometimes things are okay for a while. Rarely is it okay for the long term because of the lack of relational undergirding. It nearly always introduces an insecurity in one or both that needs a lot of reassurance—a dynamic that wasn't present before. Laying the foundation needed for a physically and emotionally safe sexual experience takes more time than most divorcees allow for.

I've heard more than once, "I wish someone had told me." Well here you are. Please take the time to search deeply within to discover your personal sexual values and take the steps to set yourself up for the kind of experience you want.

Where Are You Now?

What are your thoughts on being sexual again?

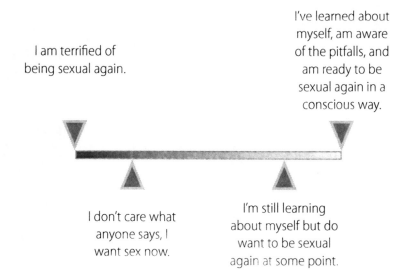

I am terrified of being sexual again.

I've learned about myself, am aware of the pitfalls, and am ready to be sexual again in a conscious way.

I don't care what anyone says, I want sex now.

I'm still learning about myself but do want to be sexual again at some point.

Part Eight

LOOKING FORWARD

30

Your New Life

*Looking back, you realize that a very special person
passed briefly through your life,
and that person was you.
It is not too late to become that person again.*

— ROBERT BRAULT

Here you are, perhaps not completely on the other side of divorce, but closer than you were, and with more understanding. You've discovered resources you didn't know you had. You've developed strengths and skills that will serve you the rest of your days. You've traversed the chasm of the In-Between Zone with its sleeping giants, steep drop-offs, and dark caverns. You've slain your dragons and now stand proudly on the head of the slain beast called "I'll Never Make It." You have made it.

You didn't know when you started where this journey would lead you. You've wondered if it would dump you out on some wasteland. You've likely had a dream for your life for many years, maybe since childhood, but for one reason or another haven't allowed yourself to dream it. It seemed too impossible, with too many obstacles, too few resources, and too many demands in other directions. As

John Lennon sang, *"Life is what happens when we're busy making other plans."* What you haven't known is that

> ## while you've been busy navigating your divorce, you've also been becoming the person who can have your dream.

Self-development and personal growth are required for us to become fully functioning adults who understand life's principles and how to work within them. Often parts of us lag behind, stuck in limbo somewhere along the growth continuum, waiting for that key ingredient to move us forward and spring us into life. Divorce is often that key ingredient. Perhaps now you are ready. You've gotten the sweet taste of personal freedom that comes with growing and changing, and you wonder how your life had meaning without it.

Your New Life

Paradigm shifts, that is moving from one reality to another, happen all around us. Some are dramatic, like the metamorphosis of caterpillar to butterfly. Some are gradual, like youth to old age. Some require a complete overhaul of habits, beliefs, and environment, like addicted to sober, overweight to thin, or married to single. None are easy. You are handed different-colored glasses through which you must view the world anew, and little looks the same. Like the hermit crab that outgrows its shell and must find another, you've outgrown your vision, or it has outgrown you. When a current vision ends, it behooves us to find another.

A paradigm shift isn't about trying to recreate what has been lost; it is about having your vision in a completely new way. When considering your future as it relates to your past, there are questions to consider. *Where are you now? Where do you want to go?* And, *What do you need to get there from here?* Everyone gets around to asking themselves these questions eventually. The answers are as individual as we are.

Two Possible Futures

Looking forward, you likely see things one of two ways. One is what you believe to be a predictable future based on what has happened up to now. The other is an unpredictable future, which is beyond what you can predict by your personal history or circumstances. Pursuing the unprecedented future requires that we be willing to look at life differently. We must shift our outlook in order to have it.

> **We must let go of the useless internal conversations, lingering resentments, and limiting self-talk so we can grab that next trapeze bar that swings just beyond our reach, waiting for us to let go of things that don't work, and stretch into the good that awaits.**

A vision is illusive. Many things will come between you and your vision. You will be required to reclaim it over and over. The same courage you found when you needed to get through your divorce will serve you in the creation of your new life. Be prepared to answer this question: *When I lose sight of my vision, what will bring me back to full participation in the creation of the future I desire?* We need our community of support not just to get through our divorce, but also to create a life worth having on the other side. Find out who is on your team.

Reclaiming Your Power

As things naturally shift and adjust to your new reality, you will push against not only your own fears and inabilities, but the fears, concerns, and sometimes wishful expectations of people around you. Reclaiming your power comes as you take one, appropriately assertive step after another, creating the space for change by setting limits on things that would encroach. As you hold to your vision of a future you love, you will discover what is next for you and define the resources you need to get there.

It takes a concerted effort to unearth a vision, declare it to the world, and make a determined commitment to do what it takes to make it a reality. Being committed to a vision will change you.

Looking Forward

Although it has helped you to keep your eyes focused forward, it is the journey itself that has been your gift. You are different now. Your friends know it. Your children know it. You are likely more at peace. Even though the circumstances of your life may still be in haphazard disarray, a calm is no doubt beginning to develop at the core of who you are. It may be hard to detect at first, seeming perhaps like the satisfaction of a good meal. But as it grows it becomes unmistakable. *"Yes. Yes. I feel it now."* Before long it will grow to include a broad smile and eventually laughter. Yes, that is your future—the freedom to be yourself.

So what does freedom mean to you? Below are a few definitions. See if you identify with any of them. After you read, you might want to write your thoughts about freedom in your journal.

Freedom is:

- being able to try out new identities, ideas, and theories.
- being able to put a fence around your yard, just because it's your yard.
- having some secret places that you don't have to share.
- being able to be yourself freely and completely—without editing—at all times.

- operating from your authentic self—
  choosing your actions, behaviors, friends,
  lovers, rules.

- ungrudgingly allowing others their freedom
  without demands or expectations that they
  be different or do different to suit you.

- taking responsibility for your needs,
  making requests for things you want, and
  being okay when someone tells you *no*.

- not losing yourself in the shadow of
  someone else, either out of your need for
  connection or another's need to control.

- not allowing anyone or anything to have
  power over you—your happiness, your
  future, your decisions, your choices.

- your power source for doing your work,
  making your impact on the planet.

- humbly accepting that you have no control
  over what someone does—to you, for you,
  or against you—knowing that your job is to
  take care of yourself while allowing others
  their choices.

- having enough space between you and an
  "other" so you don't clobber each other
  with your personal forms of wackiness.

- allowing another to be totally themselves.
  "You be you, and I'll be me. Let's walk
  along together appreciating and celebrating
  each other."

Freedom—both inward and outward, is your birth-right. It is the height of self-respect and other-respect. You've made this long and arduous journey to find your personal freedom. Now you get to live it, teach it to your kids, create from it, and enjoy others without a sense of needing something from them or demanding any kind of outcome. Freedom is yours, and no one can take that away unless you let them.

How Are You Doing?

Rate your level of freedom.

I still feel the need to be what others want me to be.

Heck yeah! Bring it on. I'm free!

I feel free to be myself most of the time.

31

Where Are You Now?

It takes a lot of courage to release the familiar
and seemingly secure, to embrace the new.
But there is no real security in what
is no longer meaningful.
There is more security in the adventurous
and exciting, for in movement there is
life, and in change there is power.

— ALAN COHEN

Think of all you've accomplished. You've done some deep emotional work, you've looked at the patterns you brought to your relationship, and you've changed what you can—for now. You've pushed yourself and, I hope, also been gentle with yourself. You've learned and grown. Perhaps a new vision is beginning to form. You're seeing yourself differently. Maybe you're surprised at the unexpected doors divorce has opened for you. Most people are.

At the start of the book you assessed the impact divorce was having on various areas of your life. Are you curious about how they've changed after all this hard work you've done? The same Wheel Assessment appears below.

Completing it will allow you to see the improvements, and the movement, you've made.

The instructions are the same: With the center as 0, as in "this area is a mess," and the outer rim as 10, meaning "there are no problems in this area," draw a line at the approximate value to represent your current level of recovery (the detailed instructions are in chapter 7). There are a few questions after the Assessment to help you best use what you learn.

Where Are You Now?

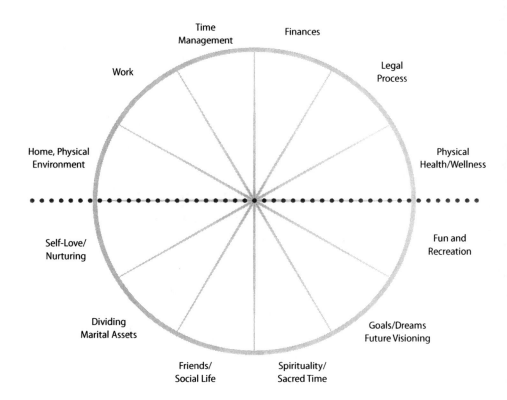

Time Management

Finances

Work

Legal Process

Home, Physical Environment

Physical Health/Wellness

Self-Love/ Nurturing

Fun and Recreation

Dividing Marital Assets

Goals/Dreams Future Visioning

Friends/ Social Life

Spirituality/ Sacred Time

Here are some questions for you to consider.

- What do you notice after completing the chart this time?
- Are there significant changes from the first time you completed it?
- Which life area is your strongest now?
- Which areas need your focus right now?

Did you identify some areas you'd like to work on? I encourage you to write in your journal or talk with a friend about an action plan with reasonable steps toward creating a life you love. When you're ready to begin you might consider hiring a coach who will help you select priorities and keep you encouraged and accountable. There are only a few things in life that are worth this kind of effort. Will you make a commitment to yourself to begin now? What is one thing you can begin tomorrow to make the changes you desire?

A Word About Failure

In wrapping up this material I want to speak to you a moment about failure. No matter how hard you try to put a positive spin on things and believe that everything will work out for the best, you will probably still have a nagging sense of failure when your relationship ends. I lived in the "if only" place for a very long time, certain that if only I'd been smarter, kinder, more loving, more forgiving, more angry, more boundaried, or found the secret that would make things all better, I could have avoided divorce and preserved my family. Perhaps you've had similar thoughts. What I've learned is that it takes two, not only to make a relationship, but also to save a relationship. No matter how much you, as a single individual could do, it would never be enough. I could not rescue my marriage, and this left me feeling like an abject failure. I felt that I'd failed my children, my parents, my God, friends, community, even my former spouse. But most of all I felt I'd failed myself.

It took me a while to understand failure as a teacher. I've come to believe that everything in life is a lesson. There are no failures, only learning. We don't figure out life without experience. What we call failing is an important part of learning any new skill. Star athletes set records not only for most homeruns or baskets made, but also the most strike-outs and missed shots.

Can you let your experience be about living, learning, and growing through all of your successes and failures? Are you willing to use your experiences to open your heart more deeply and become the person you were meant to be? If divorce is what it took for you to wake up to this opportunity to have a better life, well, hooray! Better late than never!

Can you see your life as "a dream come true" no matter what happens along the way? Life is a lot easier when you give up trying to be perfect, trying to please others, and trying to get it right. Life is inherently messy, and we have more fun once we accept that. I am grateful for the transformational journey that divorce was part of for me. I would have never gotten to the Me I know now if I'd stayed in the roles I occupied in my marriage. As in Michelangelo's sculptures, a greater Me was waiting to be released. I think you will find that true for you, too.

Until We Meet Again

I hope the information and exercises in the book have helped calm your heart and brought you into sight of a happy life again. It's a journey. Your journey. There is so much more for you to grow into and embrace about this new life—when you're ready. To that end, there will be a followup book that will take you on a journey to explore this new you in greater depth and help you move out into the world and into a future worth having.

I share my insights on these and other topics through blog articles, radio broadcasts, and speaking engagements. Please visit www.BeyondDivorce.com to learn more, and to access free resources and assessments.

I feel very privileged to walk alongside you during this leg of your journey. If I can be of any service to you, please contact me at any time.

Jeannine

Acknowledgments

Dr. Henry Cloud and Dr. John Townsend, authors of *Boundaries* and a variety of other books, have influenced many concepts in this book—the ways we grow, the ways we learn about love, and the ways we set boundaries in our relationships to protect both ourselves and love itself. Much of what I've learned has been through their written works, but I've also gleaned information from the recordings of their Monday Night Solutions and their radio presentations. Having listened to their materials for more than a dozen years, I can no longer separate my own ideas from their influence. I owe much of my understanding to these insightful men.

Dr. Bruce Fisher, in his book *Rebuilding When Your Relationship Ends*, helped me understand the commonalities in the divorce experience. My time facilitating his program opened a door I did not expect. It has given me a strong foundation for the work in this book. Todd Fisher, Dr. Fisher's oldest son, has long encouraged me to continue his father's work.

The work of The Grief Recovery Institute expanded my understanding of what it takes to move through grief in a healthy way. I have adapted some of their tools to help the divorcing people I serve. Thanks to Russell Friedman and John James for their contributions.

The Relationship Coaching Institute and David Steele, author of *Conscious Dating*, have provided many tools for singles looking for love in a conscious way, which I have adapted to help the divorcing understand what went wrong.

Books by William Bridges, the well-known transitions guru, and specifically his book *The Way of Transition*, helped put meaning and structure to my journey, which in turn helps me do the same for others.

Specific references are mentioned in the Notes section, but I name these more pervasive influences and apologize ahead of time for any material so incorporated into my own thinking that I no longer remember the source.

Notes

1. Gonzales, Laurence (2004). *Deep Survival: Who Lives, Who Dies, and Why*. New York: Norton & Company. p. 184.

2. Material provided by Dr. Ron Henry, DC, ND, FIAMA. www.newparadigmhealing.net

3. This section on natural remedies was provided by Dr. Deborah Belote, DC. www.integratedhealthcareclinic.com

4. Material provided by Dr. Ron Henry, DC, ND, FIAMA. www.newparadigmhealing.net

5. This section on natural remedies was provided by Dr. Deborah Belote, DC. www.integratedhealthcareclinic.com

6. Pema Chödrön (2000). *When Things Fall Apart*. Boston: Shambhala. p. 12.

7. James, John W., & Friedman, Russell (1998). *The Grief Recovery Handbook*. New York: Harper Perennial. p. 134.

8. Welshons, J. E. (2003). *Awakening from Grief*. Novato, CA: New World Library. [Reprinted with permission] www.newworldlibrary.com

9. This notion of "growing up" or "maturing" an emotion is one that Drs. Cloud and Townsend use. Cloud, Henry, & Townsend, John (1992). *Boundaries*. Zondervan.

10. Adapted from material by the co-founders of BEabove Leadership, Ann Betz, CPCC, and Ursula Pottinga, CPCC. www.beaboveleadership.com

11. Cori, Jasmin Lee (2010). *The Emotionally Absent Mother*. New York: The Experiment. The list that follows in the text is from pp. 109–113.

12. © Relationship Coaching Institute. [Adapted with permission]

13. I took as a model a scale by Hal and Sidra Stone published in *Embracing Your Inner Critic* (New York: HarperCollins, 1993), but have changed most items and created my own rating scale.

14. Aron, Elaine (1996). *The Highly Sensitive Person*. New York: Broadway Books. pp. 43–45.

15. This table is an adaptation of something I got from Will Limon, who was one of my mentors in the Fisher program. I am unaware of a published source.

16. Created by Craig Miller of Ventura, CA. craigm970@yahoo.com

17. The ideas for this section came from Dave Taylor, www.GoFatherhood.com, and have been paraphrased with permission.

CPSIA information can be obtained at www.ICGtesting.com
Printed in the USA
LVOW06s0606100214

373009LV00002B/2/P

9 780989 354103